THE CAPTIVE LUFTWAFFE

Part of the Captive Luftwaffe—Junkers Ju 88R-1, c/n 360043 (PJ876) and a Messerschmitt Bf 109G-2/Trop, c/n 10639 (RN228) at Horse Guards' Parade, London, in September 1954. (*John Stroud*)

THE
CAPTIVE
LUFTWAFFE

KENNETH S. WEST

PUTNAM
LONDON

© Kenneth S. West 1978
ISBN 0 370 30020 3
Printed in Great Britain for
Putnam & Company Ltd
9 Bow Street London WC2E 7AL
by BAS Printers Limited, Over Wallop
Hampshire
Set in Monophoto Times
First published in 1978

CONTENTS

Introduction

In writing this book my aim has been to provide a broad picture of the variety of captured German aircraft of the Second World War that were present in the United Kingdom during the period 1939–45 and of their evaluation. In spite of access to official and private archives during the course of fifteen years' research certain items of information still remain unconfirmed, this being indicated in the text by an asterisk. It is appreciated that some of the illustrations are of poor quality, but because of their rarity they warrant inclusion. I wish to express my thanks and appreciation for their courteous help and many practical suggestions to D. G. M. Gough; Captain E. M. Brown CBE, DSC, AFC; Air Commodore A. H. Wheeler CBE, MA, FRAeS; Mike Payne; Peter Foote; 'Russ' Snadden; Royal D. Frey; Alan Hall; Neville Franklin; Thomas H. Hitchcock; Imperial War Museum; Royal Aircraft Establishment; Newark Air Museum; and *Flight International*.

September 1977

Kenneth S. West
Bournemouth

The Royal Aircraft Establishment, Farnborough

On frequent occasions during the Second World War German aircraft literally fell upon the United Kingdom, and they subsequently arrived at experimental establishments in various stages of disrepair. Usually they were very much the worse for wear, but sometimes good fortune provided specimens in complete working order, or suffering only minor damage. Factors in securing a good flow of enemy machines were, firstly, our fighter and anti-aircraft defences but purely from the scientific viewpoint these were not over popular since they tended to inflict rather drastic damage on the specimen; the second source was primarily due to bad navigation, fuel shortage, engine failure, and defection.

The testing and evaluation of captured aircraft and equipment in the United Kingdom was undertaken by various research establishments and specialist Service units. Naturally, the Royal Aircraft Establishment at Farnborough came in the first category and was engaged in this function from 1939 to 1946. The first few enemy aircraft shot down over Britain were objects of the greatest interest and a team of experts was detailed for the sole task of examining the wrecks. The supply soon became more plentiful and it was possible, in some instances, to repair different types and put them through flight tests to determine their capabilities. After the Battle of Britain, and the subsequent bombing raids, the RAE in fact possessed a not insignificant Luftwaffe, and it was a common enough event to see mock dog-fights between British and German aircraft over Farnborough Common. The responsibility for flying captured aircraft rested on the shoulders of such distinguished test pilots as Group Captain H. J. Wilson, among others. During the course of the war several of the aircraft examined at the RAE were subsequently passed to various local and national authorities for exhibition purposes, to raise money for War Bonds and Savings, Spitfire Funds, and other causes, and some of the aircraft so exhibited are detailed in the individual aircraft history section of this book.

At the request of the Ministry of Economic Warfare, an extensive and intensive study was also undertaken of the construction methods of the German aircraft industry, in order to seek out any weaknesses in the economic and production centres. Therefore, in addition to flying aircraft

1

on test, evaluation of equipment was a primary function, various departments within the RAE being responsible for specific items. These departments, together with an example of the type of equipment tested, comprised:

AERODYNAMICS: fuel jettison system of the Junkers Ju 88.
ARMAMENTS: gun mounting and field of fire of the Ju 88.
CHEMISTRY: engine coolant used in the Heinkel He 111.
ELECTRICAL ENGINEERING: electric motor and gearbox, for engine cowl operation, of the Ju 88.
ENGINES: exhaust system of a BMW 801A from a Dornier Do 217.
INSTRUMENTS: testing Bosch magnetometer.
MATERIALS/METALS: materials of selected components of a DB 601N engine.
MECHANICAL TEST: self-sealing oil tank from a Focke-Wulf Fw 200.
PHOTOGRAPHIC: tests on a ZAK 35 mm ciné camera.
RADIO/WIRELESS: FuG 17 radio equipment from an He 111.
STRUCTURES/AIRWORTHINESS: Messerschmitt Bf 110 airframe, engines and equipment.
MISCELLANEOUS: Junkers VS 11 propeller from a Ju 88.

This equipment originated from aircraft brought down in the United Kingdom, and example aircraft, and Luftwaffe unit involved, included the following:

Dornier Do 17Z 3Z-GS of 8/KG77; Do 17Z-3 5K-AP of 6/KG3; Do 217E-1 U5-DN of 5/KG2; Do 217E-2 c/n 5437 F8-IN of 5/KG40; Do 217E-4 U5-KT of 9/KG2; Do 217M-1 c/n 56051 U5-DK of 2/KG2.

Heinkel He 111P 5J-AM of 4/KG4; He 111H-2 1H-FM of 4/KG26; He 111H-3 1H-DP of 6/KG26; He 111H-5 G1-ET of 9/KG55; He 115B 8L-EL of 3/Küstenfliegergruppe 906; He 177A-5 c/n 5747 of I/KG40.

Junkers Ju 87B-2 S2-LM of 4/St G77; Ju 88A-1 4D-AP of 6/KG30; Ju 88A-4 3E-BB of Gruppe Stab I/KG6; Ju 88C-4 R4-CH of 1/NJG2; Ju 88D-1 4U-GK of 2/Aufklärungsgruppe 123; Ju 188A-2 c/n 160069; Ju 188E-1 c/n 260171.

Messerschmitt Bf 109F-4 c/n 8453; Bf 109G-4/Trop c/n 10878; Me 210A-1 2H-CA of Geschwader Stab/Versuchsstaffel 210; Me 410 c/n 10120.

Aircraft that were flown on test and evaluation at the RAE and operated by the Aerodynamics Flight included, at various periods: Focke-Wulf Fw 190A-3 MP499; Fw 190A-4/U8 PE882; Fw 190A-5/U8 PM679; Gotha Go 145B BV207; Heinkel He 111H-1 AW177; He 162A-2 VH513; He 177A-5/R6 TS439; Junkers Ju 88A-1 AX919; Ju 88A-5 EE205; Ju 88G-1 TP190; Ju 88R-1 PJ876; Messerschmitt Bf 109E-3 AE479; Bf 109F-2 ES906; Bf 109G-6/U2 TP814; Bf 110C-5 AX772; Me 262A-2a VK893; Me 410A-3 TF209.

See the individual aircraft history section for complete details.

At the end of hostilities there was a large influx of captured enemy

2

Messerschmitt Bf 109E-3 cockpit layout.

hardware, some of which was subsequently displayed at the Captured
Enemy Aircraft Exhibition, Farnborough, during October/November
1945, the aircraft being collected from various Continental airfields, and
later some were shipped to the Dominions and the USA. More than 150
machines were brought to the United Kingdom for examination,
evaluation and test. Eventually the majority passed to No. 6 MU Brize
Norton and No. 47 MU Sealand for storage and/or shipment, although a
great number of these aircraft were destroyed at No. 6 MU during the
winter gales of 1946–47.

No. 1426 (EAC) Flight in about 1943. *Back row,* left to right; Messrs Fendley, Rylatt, AC1 J. G. Lambert, Messrs Seddon, Craven, Wyles, Ochiltree. *Middle row;* AC1 W. T. Haley, Mr Lovell, AC2 A. Fraser, Mr Hodson, AC1 J. W. Shufflebotham, Messrs Felton, Westwood, Hearne, Henshaw, Wilson, Driver, Aircraftman Aslett, Mr Frisby. *Front row,* seated; Cpl Keeble, Cpl Peat, Flt/Sgt Bennet, Pilot Officer F. A. Barr, Flying Officer D. G. M. Gough, Flt Lt R. F. Forbes, Flying Officer E. R. Lewendon, Flying Officer Staples, Sgt W. Dowie, Cpls Ellis. Unfortunately the ranks and initials of many in this photograph cannot be traced. Heinkel He 111H-1 AW177 is in the background.

No. 1426 (Enemy Aircraft) Flight

The main specialist Service unit which operated captured enemy aircraft, expressly to exhibit them to operational units in the British Isles, to give ground and flying demonstrations for the benefit of ground staff, aircrew and aerodrome defence personnel, and for fighter liaison and aircraft recognition duties, was formed at RAF Duxford on 21 November, 1941. The initial personnel consisted of Flying Officer R. F. Forbes, the first Commanding Officer, Flying Officer Kinder, Pilot Officer E. R. Lewendon and Flt/Sgt D. G. M. Gough, all being posted from the Air Fighting Development Unit (AFDU) to which they had been attached for eleven days for flying experience on German aircraft. All the pilots had previously been in No. 41 Group as Maintenance Unit test pilots. The Flight came under the operational control of No. 12 Group, Fighter Command.

The first aircraft allotted was the Heinkel He 111H-1 AW177 from the RAE, on 7 December, 1941, followed by the Messerschmitt Bf 109E-3 AE479 and the Junkers Ju 88A-5 HM509 on 11 December, 1941. The posting of maintenance personnel began on 22 December, 1941, and some of the ground crews were sent to the RAE for instruction in the maintenance of German aircraft. An addition to the Flight on 2 February,

1942, was Flt/Sgt F. A. Barr, who was posted to the unit for full flying duties.

No. 1 tour of RAF stations began on 11 February, 1942, and flying demonstrations were given at Lakenheath, Watton, Coltishall, Bircham Newton, Docking, Sutton Bridge and Wittering. On 5 March, 1942, Messerschmitt Bf 110C-5 AX772 was posted-in from the Royal Navy AFDU. No. 2 tour started on 1 April, 1942, and demonstrations were given at RAF stations North Luffenham, Cottesmore, Saltby, Cranwell, Digby, Waddington, Hemswell, Kirton-in-Lindsey, North Coates and Snaith. On 28 April, 1942, Messerschmitt Bf 109E-3 DG200 was delivered by road in a dismantled condition. No. 3 tour began on 4 May, 1942, and covered RAF stations Church Fenton, Holme-on-Spalding Moor, Breighton, Leconfield, Catfoss, Driffield, Pocklington, Marston Moor, Linton-upon-Ouse and Dishforth. No. 4 tour followed on 15 June, 1942, to RAF stations Cranfield, Bassingbourne, Twinwood, Waterbeach, Stradishall, Newmarket, Wattisham, Debden, Castle Camps, North Weald,

Flt Lt E. R. Lewendon (left) and Flying Officer D. G. M. Gough.

Hornchurch, Bradwell Bay, Fairlop, West Malling, Detling and return to Duxford on 3 July, 1942. Meanwhile, on 12 June, 1942, Junkers Ju 88A-1s AX919 and HX360 arrived by road from the RAE and were used as a source of spares to service HM509 and EE205. On 25 July, 1942, No. 5 tour visited Biggin Hill, Gravesend, Kenley, Redhill, Atcham, Heston, Northolt, Aircraft and Armament Experimental Establishment (A & AEE) Boscombe Down, where test pilots flew the aircraft, and the Ju 88 HM509 was flown at night for exhaust glare photographs. The tour continued to USAAF stations Bovingdon and Molesworth. The Junkers Ju 88A-5 EE205 was flown in from the RAE on 28 August, 1942, and No. 6 tour began on 4 September, 1942, to USAAF station Atcham and RAF stations Ibsley, Old Sarum, Andover and Colerne. Continuing the 'merry round', No. 7 tour on 14 October, 1942, covered Charmy Down, Weston Zoyland, Church Stanton, Exeter, Harrowbeer, Chivenor, Netheravon, Hullavington and Castle Combe. No. 8 tour, on 30 November, 1942, visited Aston Down, Chedworth, South Cerney, Abingdon, Bicester, Upper Heyford, Chipping Warden and Bovingdon. During January 1943 the Bf 110 AX772 was flown on ground strafing exercises for the RAF Regiment. On 24 February, 1943, No. 9 tour began and visits were made to USAAF stations Debden, Castle Camps, Bassingbourne, Thurleigh, Chelveston, Molesworth, Alconbury, Honington, Hardwick, Bungay, Shipdham, Horsham St Faith, Swanton Morley, Foulsham, West Raynham, Great Massingham, returning to Duxford on 9 April, 1943, the unit meanwhile having moved to RAF Collyweston on 12 March, 1943. On 27 May, 1943, the Flight went to RAF Digby and was inspected by King George VI and Queen Elizabeth.

Flt/Sgt D. G. M. Gough and Messerschmitt Bf 109E-3 AE479 at RAF Duxford on 2 January, 1942.

Henschel Hs 129B-1 NF756 arrived in packing cases on 27 June, 1943. On 7 July, 1943, the He 111H-1 AW177 and one of the Ju 88s was flown to USAAF station Polebrook to enable Captain Clark Gable to make an instructional film for air gunners. On 10 August, 1943, some members of the Enemy Aircraft Non-Ferrous Materials Committee and representatives of High Duty Alloys visited the Flight to study the materials and construction of the Hs 129. Messerschmitt Bf 109F-4/B NN644 was received, via the RAE, on 21 August, 1943, followed on 28 September by the Focke-Wulf Fw 190A-4/U8 PN 999, also from RAE. October 1943 saw the arrival of some Polish aircrew, who were taught to fly the German aircraft, and on 5 November, 1943, the Bf 109F-4/B NN644 was flown for air-to-air photography in company with a Hudson, flown by Flt Capt James Mollison of the Air Transport Auxiliary.

No. 10 tour began on 6 November, 1943, consisting of He 111H-1 AW177, Ju 88A-5 HM509 and Bf 109F-4/B NN644, visiting USAAF stations Goxhill, Grafton Underwood and arriving at Polebrook on 10 November. Up to this time the Flight had not experienced a serious accident but while landing at Polebrook the He 111 and Ju 88 used the same runway from opposite ends and when the pilot of the Heinkel, Flying Officer F. A. Barr, saw the Ju 88 approaching, he opened up the engines and did a steep turn to port, stalled, and spun-in vertically. Seven of the eleven on board were killed when the fuel tanks exploded on impact.

On 12 December, 1943, two Fw 190s, NF754 and NF755, arrived, and on 26 December Messerschmitt Bf 109G-2/Trop RN228 followed, all in packing cases via the Middle East and Liverpool Docks. No. 11 tour began on 31 December, 1943, and visited USAAF stations Molesworth, Chelveston, Kimbolton, Thurleigh, Poddington, Bassingbourne, Steeple Morden and Cheddington, returning to Collyweston on 1 February, 1944. Messerschmitt Bf 109G-6/Trop VX101 arrived on 4 February, and on 23 March No. 12 tour began to RAF and USAAF stations Hullavington, Bovingdon, Chipping Ongar, Stansted, Great Dunmow, Great Sailing, Earls Colne, Rivenhall, Ridgewell, Wattisham, Boxted, Raydon, Martlesham Heath and Framlingham, returning to Collyweston on 5 May.

Focke-Wulf Fw 190A-4/U8 PE882 arrived from the RAE on 23 April, 1944, followed on 6 May by the Junkers Ju 88R-1 PJ876. On 9 May the Flight moved to RAF Thorney Island, for five weeks' attachment, for recognition exercises over the invasion fleet on the south coast. The Flight began a special recognition exercise for the Mosquito squadrons based at RAF West Raynham and Little Snoring on 9 August, 1944. During the preceding month, on 11 July, the Focke-Wulf Fw 190A-5/U8 PM 679 arrived by road from the AFDU Wittering, to be used as a source of spares to service PN999. On 18 September, 1944, the Flight's aircraft were flown to USAAF Chipping Ongar, where they were used for instructional purposes by the USAAF Disarmament School, for the maintenance and temporary immobilisation of German aircraft.

No. 1426 line-up at RAF Collyweston on 15 February, 1944. *Left to right*; Henschel Hs 129B-1 NF756, Focke-Wulf Fw 190A-4 PN999, Messerschmitt Bf 109G-2/Trop RN228, Messerschmitt Bf 110C-5 AX772 and Junkers Ju 88A-5 EE205.

Left to right; Flt/Sgt Lee, Flying Officer Staples, Flying Officer D. G. M. Gough and Flt Lt E. R. Lewendon at RAF Collyweston in October 1944. Lewendon is wearing a Luftwaffe pilot's badge on his left breast pocket. Messerschmitt Bf 110C-5 AX772 is in the background.

On 25 September, 1944, the Junkers Ju 88S-1 TS472 arrived from Villacoublay, and on 27 September Flt Lt R. F. Forbes was posted from the Flight to No. 61 OTU. Flt Lt E. R. Lewendon had succeeded him as CO that August. On 13 October, 1944, while doing local flying in Fw 190A-4/U8 PE882, Lewendon was killed when the aircraft crashed. With effect from 14 October, Flt Lt D. G. M. Gough assumed command of the unit. On 5 December, 1944, the Ju 88S-1 TS472 was flown on an affiliation exercise with a Lancaster from RAF Woolfox, followed on 18 December by recognition exercises at RAF Ossington; also on 14 January, 1945, a Ju 88 was flown to RAF Kenley, by Flt/Sgt Bennett, for exercises on the temporary immobilisation and maintenance of German aircraft. On 19 January, 1945, a working party was flown to Deurne (Antwerp) to collect two Messerschmitt Bf 109G-14/U4s, VD358 and VD364, although these aircraft were subsequently used by the Enemy Aircraft Flight (EAF), Central Fighter Establishment (CFE), RAF Tangmere, because on 21 January official notification was received of the disbandment of No. 1426 (EAC) Flight with effect from 17 January, 1945. During the three years and two months of its existence it had met with many maintenance difficulties, due to the lack of spares and maintenance details. Tools and equipment had to be specially made, and all engine and airframe spares obtained from crashed and unserviceable aircraft. It was also necessary to assemble aircraft that had never been in the United Kingdom and about which little was known from a maintenance point of view.

8

Other Operators of Captured Enemy Aircraft

In addition to the two main operators, the RAE Farnborough and No. 1426 (EAC) Flight, the Aeroplane & Armament Experimental Establishment, Boscombe Down, was also involved with evaluation trials on aircraft and equipment during 1940-45, specifically the Heinkel He 111H-1 AW177, Messerschmitt Bf 109E-3 AE 479, Junkers Ju 88G c/n 622138, Ju 88R-1 PJ876, and the Ju 188 c/n 280032.

The Air Fighting Development Unit, RAF Northolt, Duxford and Wittering, and the Royal Navy AFDU, operated the aircraft on comparison and evaluation flights against current Allied aircraft and equipment. The Airborne Forces Experimental Establishment at RAF Beaulieu specialised in trials of the Focke Achgelis Fa 330 and Fa 223, the latter being the first helicopter to be flown across the English Channel. Another specialist unit, the Marine Aircraft Experimental Establishment, at RAF Helensburgh and Felixstowe, used captured examples of the Arado Ar 196, Blohm und Voss Bv 138 and Bv 222, Dornier Do 24, and the Junkers Ju 52/3m floatplane on evaluation flights. As the name implies, the Fighter Interception Development Unit operated selected examples on comparative radio and radar interception technique trials, including the Junkers Ju 88G Air Ministry 33.

Tribute should be paid to the pilots who undertook the flight testing of captured German aircraft at the experimental stations. As may well be imagined, even when it was known that precautions had been taken against untoward incidents, flying an enemy aircraft over Britain, while concentrating on instruments and accuracy of flying during performance and handling tests, was not conducive to peace of mind.

Readers should refer to the individual aircraft histories for reference to specific users and dates.

Identification Systems

British aircraft serials were allotted primarily to those aircraft which were allocated to test and evaluation flying programmes. Serials were issued, as and when required, in the normal current sequences, the first being AE479 to a Bf 109E-3, in June 1940, and the final allotment VX190 to the Brunswick Zaunkönig, in about 1946.

In 1945-46, when the large influx of captured enemy material occurred for technical evaluation, the Air Ministry allocated numbers between 1 and 250, with the prefix Air Min, or just AM, to specific airframes. Additionally, and for now unknown reasons, the Air Ministry allocated to

Me 410 aircraft a series of V numbers, *eg*, Air Ministry V3 was an Me 410B-6. As a rule the Air Ministry numbers were crudely applied to the aircraft in white or black paint on the rear fuselage, aft of the roundel, usually on the port side only, but there were exceptions to this practice, although at least one machine, Bf 110G-4/R7, c/n 730037, had the number painted neatly and in full, as AIR MINISTRY 30, for the benefit of official publicity photographs. The highest known allotment is Air Ministry 231, a Ju 88G-1, but it should be noted that although numbers were allocated to specific aircraft, these numbers were not necessarily applied to the airframe. Additionally, an aircraft could be allocated an Air Ministry number but if it was subsequently required for test flying a normal serial allocation was made in addition.

Enemy Aircraft numbers were allocated by the Enemy Aircraft Flight, Central Fighter Establishment, Tangmere, early in 1945, when captured enemy aircraft were acquired subsequent to the demise of No. 1426 (EAC) Flight. The letters EA preceded the roundel, which was followed by a number, although very few allocations are known.

Although very little is known about the system, it would appear that the General Duties Flight at the Royal Aircraft Establishment, Farnborough, allocated a series of numbers to specific aircraft operated by them, *eg* GD1 was a Ju 52/3m.

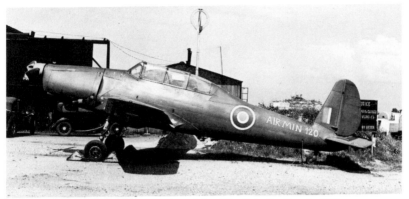

Arado Ar 96B Air Ministry 120 at Woodley, Reading, in 1946.

Individual Aircraft Histories

Arado

Ar 96B

At least three examples of this two-seat training aircraft were captured, and were at Woodley, near Reading, during 1945–47. They were allotted Air Ministry numbers 120, 121 and 123. Additionally one airframe is believed to have been allocated serial VM761.

Ar 196A-1

This specific example of the standard catapult seaplane of the Kriegsmarine, carrying the T3 code of Bordfliegerstaffeln 1/196 or 5/196, from the *Admiral Hipper*, was captured early in the Norwegian campaign and handed over to the British forces. It was flown to the United Kingdom but crashed on 26 April, 1940, on alighting at Rhu on the Gare Loch, near the Marine Aircraft Experimental Establishment (MAEE), Helensburgh, the pilot, Commander C. W. Byas, RN, being injured as the aircraft overturned.

Ar 196

An example was evaluated at the MAEE in about 1945–46, receiving Air Ministry number 92 and serial VM748.

11

Arado Ar 196 Air Ministry 92. (*Newark Air Museum 3769*)

Ar 232B-0

This four-engined transport, originally R-B of 3/KG200, was surrendered to the RAF at an aerodrome north of Hamburg, and flown to the Royal Aircraft Establishment (RAE), Farnborough, by a Feldwebel Funk, being exhibited there in October/November 1945. Allotted Air Ministry number 17, the aircraft was finished in two shades of mottled grey, with pale blue-grey undersurfaces.

Arado Ar 232B-0 Air Ministry 17 at the RAE on 27 September, 1946, with the elephant-carrier motif on the nose. (*RAE*)

Ar 232B-0

This unidentified example was experimentally fitted with a boundary layer control system, and was retained by the Arado Flugzeugwerke as a transport for the support of the Ar 234 jet bomber test programme. It was surrendered to the RAF at the end of hostilities and flown to the United Kingdom.

12

Ar 234

At least eleven examples of this, the world's first operational turbojet bomber/reconnaissance aircraft, were examined and evaluated in the United Kingdom. They were captured at Karup (Grove), Denmark, and Stavanger (Sola), Norway, and had been operated by 1(F)/33 and Einsatz Kommando 1(F)/5. Additionally, some aircraft captured intact at Leck, Schleswig-Holstein, in May 1945 had been operated by KG76, in particular that of the Geschwaderkommodore, Oberst-leutnant Robert Kowalewski, whose aircraft, a B-2 sub-type, coded F1-AA, with individual number 13, was captured at Achmer. A total of nine, including seven from Stavanger, were flown to the RAE, via Schleswig for refuelling, by Sq Ldr A. F. Martindale, Lt-Cmdr E. M. Brown and Hauptmann Miersch. The first to land at the RAE arrived via Tangmere, where it had cleared customs, on 6 June, 1945. Air Ministry 25 and 26 followed on 25 June, a further pair on 9 July, with final deliveries that October. All these aircraft were serviced at the RAE by Hauptmann Miersch and Feldwebels Walter Rautenberg and Walter Renner, all ex-Luftwaffe personnel.

Ar 234B-1 (c/n 140008)

Flown from Karup (Grove) to the RAE, via Schleswig, by Lt-Cmdr E. M. Brown on 25 June, 1945, subsequently receiving Air Ministry number 25 and serial VK880. It was at No. 6 Maintenance Unit (MU) Brize Norton from 22 July to 30 November, 1945.

Ar 234B-1 (c/n 140113)

Flown from the RAE to No. 6 MU Brize Norton, by Lt-Cmdr E. M. Brown on 7 September, 1945. Allocated Air Ministry number 54 and VH530, it was still in storage at No. 6 MU on 21 March, 1946.

Ar 234B-2 (c/n 140141)

Flown from the RAE to No. 6 MU Brize Norton, for storage, by Lt-Cmdr E. M. Brown on 15 October, 1945.

Ar 234B-2 (c/n 140173)

F1-MT, individual letter M, of 9/KG76 based at Rheine. The first example captured by the Allies, it had suffered a flame-out in one engine and was forced-down by P-47 Thunderbolts of the US Ninth Air Force near the village of Segelsdorf at 11.00 on 24 February, 1945. The aircraft was virtually intact, suffering minor damage only to the nose and cockpit. Detailed examination showed that it had been hit by several 0·5-inch bullets, which had lodged in the wings and fuselage. The turbojets, which were later examined by Sir Frank Whittle's Power Jets (Research & Development) Ltd, were the first to be captured in full working order. After preliminary examination on site the aircraft was dismantled and shipped to the RAE for detailed scrutiny on 21 March, 1945, but it was not flown.

Ar 234B-2 (c/n 140466)

This aircraft, allocated Air Ministry 24, crashed on its ferry flight, at Farnborough, on 27 August, 1945.

Arado Ar 234B-2, c/n 140493, at Wisley. (*IWM MH4870*)

Ar 234B-2 (c/n 140493)

Individual number 5. At the RAE and Wisley during 1945, subsequently in storage at No. 6 MU Brize Norton on 30 November, 1945, it had shiny dark green upper surfaces and pale blue undersurfaces.

Ar 234B-2 (c/n 140581)

Flown from Stavanger (Sola) to Schleswig, via Karup (Grove) on 24 September, 1945; to Nordholz on 3 October, and to the RAE on 27 October by Lt-Cmdr E. M. Brown.

Ar 234B-2b (c/n 140476)

Individual letter D of 1(F)/33 based at Karup (Grove). Flown from Karup (Grove) to the RAE, via Schleswig, by Sq Ldr A. F. Martindale on 25 June, 1945, allocated Air Ministry number 26 and VK877. It was flown to No. 6 MU Brize Norton, for storage, on 7 October, 1945, but appeared at the RAE exhibition in October/November 1945. It had mottled grey and green upper surfaces and pale blue undersurfaces.

Arado Ar 234B-2b, c/n 140476, at the RAE in about 1945. (*RAE*)

Ar 234 (c/n 140356)

Flown from Stavanger (Sola) to Karup (Grove) on 23 September, 1945; to Schleswig on 25 September; to Brussels (Melsbroek) on 6 October, and finally to the RAE on 7 October by Lt-Cmdr E. M. Brown.

Ar 234 (c/n 140596)

At the RAE during 1945, no further details available.

The five aircraft 140141, 140356, 140493, 140581 and 140596 were allocated Air Ministry numbers 80, 226, 227, 228 and 229, and one had serial VK874, but to which specific airframes the numbers applied is not known. Additionally, Air Ministry 80 had been previously allotted to Messerschmitt Me 262A-2a, c/n 111690.

Ar 240

An example of this twin-engined two-seat long-range reconnaissance aircraft was reported at the RAE on 12 September, 1945, but no further information has, so far, been discovered.

Blohm und Voss

Bv 138B-1

Three examples of this three-engined reconnaissance flying-boat were captured at Trondheim, Norway, and flown to the United Kingdom. It was, incidentally, the only Blohm und Voss design to achieve quantity production status during the Second World War. The three were allotted Air Ministry 52/VK895, VN887 and Air Ministry 70/VM743*, the last having c/n 310081. The aircraft were evaluated at the MAEE Helensburgh

* Unconfirmed

and Felixstowe during 1945–47, with black upper and side surfaces, dark blue wing undersurfaces and small RAF roundels on the tail booms and beneath the wing.

Bv 155 V3

Originally designated Me 155, this single-seat high-altitude interceptor, a B-series prototype, was captured in a semi-completed condition, at Hamburg (Finkenwerder) in May 1945, and shipped to the RAE for examination and exhibition, with natural metal finish and without markings. It was subsequently shipped to the USA, receiving Foreign Equipment number FE-505. It is in storage for the Smithsonian Institution.

Blohm und Voss Bv 155 V3, at the RAE in November 1945. (*RAE*)

Bv 222C-012

This six-engined flying-boat, originally designed for maritime patrol and reconnaissance but later used in the transport role, was captured at Trondheim, and flown to RAF Calshot on 17 July, 1945, by Group Captain Alan F. Hards, DSO, an extensive handling test flight following on 24 July by the same pilot. It was subsequently evaluated by the MAEE Felixstowe and by No. 201 Squadron at Calshot in 1945–46, finally being broken-up at the latter base in 1947. The aircraft was allotted Air Ministry number 138, although it is doubtful that this was ever carried, and was flown with serial VP501 and a blue R ahead of the roundel. The overall finish was mottled light and dark grey on upper surfaces with light blue undersurfaces.

Blohm und Voss Bv 222C-012 VP501 at Calshot in about 1945.

Brunswick LF 1 Zaunkönig V2 D-YBAR at the RAE. (*IWM MH4914*)

Brunswick

LF 1 Zaunkönig V2

Although strictly not ex-Luftwaffe, this STOL light aircraft was built by the students at the Brunswick Technical High School and first flew in April 1945 at Bad Harzburg. After capture it was shipped to the United Kingdom and was first flown at the RAE, with German civil registration D-YBAR, on 18 September, 1947, by Lt-Cmdr E. M. Brown. It was later allotted serial VX190. The aircraft came onto the United Kingdom civil register as G-ALUA, and in 1974 went to Ireland where it was registered EI-AYU. It was still in existence at the end of 1976.

Brunswick Zaunkönig V2, as G-ALUA of the Ultra Light Aircraft Association.

17

Bücker Bü 131B Jungmann, c/n 4477, at Somerford in May 1941. (*IWM FF2*)

Bücker

Bü 131B Jungmann (c/n 4477)

GD-EG of Luftdienst. This two-seat trainer was stolen from the enemy-held aerodrome at Caen in France by two ex-Armée de l'Air pilots, Heberd and Bergerac, on 29 April, 1941, and flown to the United Kingdom. Intercepted by Allied fighters, the aircraft landed at Somerford, Christchurch, and was allotted the serial DR626 in May. On 22 May the trainer was dismantled and sent to London by road for War Weapons Week display, still in Luftwaffe markings, returning to Christchurch on 13 June. It was found that the aircraft was so extensively damaged by souvenir hunters that it had to be struck off charge on 5 November, 1941.

Bü 180 Student

Only one example of this single-engined two-seat trainer arrived in the United Kingdom, and it was exhibited at the RAE in November 1945, allotted Air Ministry number 53.

Bü 181C-3 Bestmann (c/n 120417)

This single-engined two-seat trainer was used by the General Duties Flight, RAE, in the communication/transport role, arriving at Farnborough on 1 November, 1945. On 10 July, 1947, it was registered G-AKAX but never flown as such, and was broken-up at Denham in about 1950.

Bücker Bü 181C-3 Bestmann G-AKAX at Denham.

Bü 181 Bestmann

The following were operated on communication/transport duties during 1945–46:

VM143, VM148, VM151, VM157, VM162, VM169, VM174, VM179, VM181, VM188, VM193, VM199, VM206, VM213, VM215 (Villacoublay, France, July 1946), VM220, VM227 (c/n 120502), VM231 (c/n 120222), VM238, VM243 (c/n 120508), VM252, VM259, VM263, VM269, VM274, VM278, VM401 (reported but serial not officially allocated), VM659 (reported but serial allocated to a Slingsby glider), VM768–VM770, VM771 (c/n 210208), VM772 (c/n 120518), VM773–VM785, VM786 (c/n 502061), VM787, VM788 (c/n 120520), VM789 (c/n 331563), VM790 (c/n 120071), VM791 (c/n 331319), VM792 (c/n 111192), VM793–VM796, VN169–VN175, VN782 (c/n 331303), VN783 (c/n 177), VN784 (c/n 6384), VN785 (c/n 120519), VN786 (c/n 258), VN787 (c/n 301659).

Deutsches Forschungsinstitut für Segelflug (DFS)

A number of gliders of German manufacture were in Britain before the Second World War, but the following were acquired after the cessation of hostilities, and are relevant to this book:

DFS 108-14 Schulgleiter SG 38: VP559–VP582
DFS 108-30 Kranich: Built by Jacobs-Schweyer. VP591/RAFGSA 271, later BGA 1258. VS208 was another example.
DFS 108-49 Grunau Baby: Built by J. G. Schneider. VN148 (originally LN-ST and later BAPC 33), VP587, VS220, VT762.
DFS 108-70 Meise: Originally LF-VO, later allocated VS201.
DFS Stummel-Habicht (Hawk): Built by Wolf Hirth, Nabern (Teck). This 20-ft span high-wing-loading glider, used by the NSFK (National Sozialistisch Flieger Korps) trainees destined to fly the Me 163, Me 262 or He 162, was first flown on 22 May, 1943, at Nabern. It was at the RAE in about 1945.

One of the only two DFS 228s.

DFS 228V1: One of the most important, and exotic, aircraft was this rocket-powered high-altitude reconnaissance sailplane, which was captured intact at Horsching, near Ainring, Upper Austria, in 1945. Finished in high gloss cream overall, it carried the German civil registration D-IBFQ, and was subsequently shipped to the RAE, suffering considerable damage in transit and with much of the internal equipment missing. Later it was transferred to Slingsby Sailplanes Ltd, for examination, probably in 1946, and subsequently shipped to Wright Field, USA.

Dornier

Do 17P

5D-JL of 3(F)/31. This aircraft took-off from its base at St Brieuc at 09.00 on 27 August, 1940, on a photographic reconnaissance mission to cover the St Eval and Plymouth areas. About an hour and a half after take-off it was attacked by Hurricanes of No. 238 Squadron, flown by Flt Lt M. V. Blake and Pilot Officer B. B. Considine, and forced to crash land at Hurdwick Farm, a mile north-northwest of Tavistock in Devon. The crew,

Dornier Do 17P 5D-JL on display at Salisbury.

comprising Leutnant Walter Hoffa, Feldwebel Gunther Klaushenke and Gefreiter Johannes Schesjel, was taken prisoner and the aircraft sent to the RAE for examination. Later this Do 17P was exhibited, without engines, at Salisbury and in Dean Park, Bournemouth.

Do 17Z-3

U5-LK of 2/KG2. This aircraft took-off from its base at Epinoy at 13.30 on 26 August, 1940, to attack Rochford aerodrome, near Southend. The objective reached, at 1,600 ft the Dornier was attacked by Spitfires. In their first pass the Spitfires damaged the port engine and in their second attack damaged the flying controls and destroyed the compass. Finally the starboard engine was damaged, and at 15.00 the Dornier made a forced landing on Rochford aerodrome. The Dornier's crew comprised Hauptmann Hans Bose (pilot), Obergefreiter Roeder (observer), Unteroffizier Eilert Schmidt (wireless operator) and Unteroffizier Theodor Lunghard (flight engineer). Only the observer was badly wounded.

The aircraft was sent to the RAE for examination, and then placed in storage for postwar exhibition. It was still crated at the Air Historical Branch's store at RAF Fulbeck in about 1950, but is believed to have been scrapped. The aircraft's code letters were black outlined in white.

Do 24T

Three examples of this three-engined transport/reconnaissance flying-boat were flown to the United Kingdom, being evaluated at the MAEE Felixstowe in about 1945–47. They were all from Seenotgruppen 80 or 81, based at Grossenbrode, c/n 1135 being allocated Air Ministry number 114/VN865*, c/n 3435 Air Ministry 118*/VN870*, and the third example being VM483. All were finished in black overall. After evaluation one aircraft was used, in the summer of 1946, as a target for RAF fighter firing practice, and although heavily damaged it failed to sink, being finally scuttled off Sylt by an explosive charge. It has been reported that the forward hull, including gun cupola, of one of these aircraft is at Henlow.

Do 217M-1 (c/n 56158)

From KG2. Test flown at Schleswig on 24/25 August, 1945, by Lt-Cmdr E. M. Brown, subsequently being flown to the United Kingdom and allocated Air Ministry number 107, full handling trials being undertaken at the RAE, by the same pilot, on 18 October, 1945. The aircraft was exhibited at the RAE in November, with the same finish as Air Ministry 106 (*see over*), and flown to No. 6 MU Brize Norton on 29 December, 1945,

*Unconfirmed.

Dornier Do 217M-1 Air Ministry 107 at the RAE in November 1945. (*RAE*)

Pilot's position in a Do 217M-1, From a German handbook.

passing to No. 47 MU Sealand, for storage, on 25 September, 1946. This example was also intended for postwar exhibition but was scrapped at No. 71 MU Bicester in about 1956.

Do 217M-1 (c/n 56527)

U5-HK of 2/KG2. Exhibited at the RAE in October/November 1945 and allocated Air Ministry 106. It was distempered matt black overall with snaky grey mottling.

Do 335A-0

This tandem-engined single-seat fighter was originally captured by the USAAF at Rheims. It was handed over to the RAF and test flown on its behalf by Hauptmann Miersch on 9 December, 1945, and by Lt-Cmdr E. M. Brown on 12 December, being subsequently flown to Merville, France, by Miersch on its delivery flight to the RAE on 13 December. Due to hydraulic trouble, which prevented the nosewheel being lowered, the aircraft was damaged in the subsequent forced-landing. Its ultimate fate is unknown. Although provisionally allocated Air Ministry 223 there is no evidence that this identification was ever carried.

Do 335A-12 (c/n 240112)

This two-seat dual-control trainer version was captured at Oberpfaffenhofen by United States troops and subsequently handed over to the RAF. First test flown by Sq Ldr McCarthy on 7 September, 1945, and flown the same day to Rheims by Flt Lt Taylor. On the following day it was flown to the RAE, via Manston, by Sq Ldr McCarthy. A general handling test flight, by Wing Cmdr 'Roly' Falk, took place on 1 October. During a familiarization flight on 18 January, 1946, the rear engine caught fire and the elevator controls burnt through, causing the aircraft to plunge vertically into a school-house at Cove, Hampshire, killing Group Captain

Dornier Do 335A-12, c/n 240112, at the RAE, with RAF roundel superimposed on the USAAF insignia. (*RAE*)

Alan F. Hards, DSO, CO of the RAE, who had no time to bale out. Although allocated Air Ministry 225 this identification was never carried. The aircraft had dark green mottled upper surfaces and silver-grey under-surfaces and nose-engine cowling.

Fieseler

Fi 103, FZG 76, V1, Reichenberg IV

This single-seat piloted version of the V1 was exhibited at the RAE in October/November, 1945, with mottled green-grey top surfaces and blue undersurfaces. Numerous Reichenberg IVs are on exhibition in the United Kingdom but these are all faked replicas, the RAE aircraft being the only genuine example. Its ultimate fate is unknown.

Fieseler Reichenberg IV at the RAE in November 1945. (*Flight International 18996S*)

Fi 156 Storch (Stork)

Numerous examples of this STOL general communications/reconnaissance aircraft were captured and operated in the United Kingdom and on the Continent.

HK 986, HK987 (c/n 156), VG919 (c/n 130 built as part of a Luftwaffe contract by Morane-Saulnier at Puteaux, near Paris. To A & AEE October 1945), VH751, VH752–753 (attached BAFO Communications Flight), VH754–756 (attached Supreme HQ), VM291 (c/n 779), VM292 (c/n 1576), VM293 (c/n 2010), VM294 (c/n 1665), VM295 (c/n 5746), VM296 (c/n 2547. These last six aircraft were attached to No. 83 Group's Communication Squadron), VM472 (attached to GOC 21st Army Group),

The interior of Fieseler Fi 156C-1 VP546.

VM489 (attached to No. 26 Squadron), VM824–VM846, VM874 (attached to No. 84 Group's Communication Squadron 25 October, 1945, with No. 412 Repair and Salvage Unit 12 April, 1946, destroyed and struck off charge 21 June, 1946. The serial, VM874, was previously allotted to a Ju 88), VM897–VM898, VN266 (c/n 5987), VN267 (c/n 5388), VN877, VX154 (coded HB as Air Vice-Marshal Sir Harry Broadhurst's aircraft, and originally blue overall, later camouflaged dark green and dark earth).

Air Ministry 90, Air Ministry 100 appeared at the RAE Exhibition in October/November 1945 and c/n 2008, coded CV-KB, was possibly operated by No. 3 Squadron RAAF in the Middle East.

Fi 156C-1 (c/n 475081)

Operated by the Aerodynamics Flight, RAE, during the period 1945–56, being allocated Air Ministry 101/VP546. During this period it was flown onto and off the aircraft-carrier HMS *Triumph* on 28 and 29 May, 1946, by Lt-Cmdr E. M. Brown, during a sortie from RNAS Ford. Subsequently allotted the Maintenance Command serial 7362M, and displayed at various RAF stations in the United Kingdom. At varying times has carried codes RR-KE, 101, and GM-AK. This aircraft was still at St Athan in 1976.

Fieseler Fi 156C-1 VP546, with silver overall finish.

Fieseler Fi 156C-1 GM-AK at RAF Coltishall in about 1965.

Fieseler Fi 156C-3 VD-TD (Air Ministry 99) at the RAE in 1945. (*IWM MH4913*)

Fi 156C-3

This aircraft, VD-TD, was flown from Knokke/le Zoute to the RAE on 5 September, 1945, with a refuelling stop at RAF Hawkinge, It went to No. 47 MU Sealand for crating in May 1946, was allocated Air Ministry 99, and sent to Cape Town, arriving their on 6 November, 1946. The aircraft is now in the Saxonwold Museum, Johannesburg.

Flettner

Fl 282B Kolibri (Humming-bird) (c/n 28368)

Built at the Flettner Flugzeugbau's Johannisthal factory, this twin intermeshing two-blade rotor helicopter was shipped to the United Kingdom in about 1945. The Fl 282 was extremely manoeuvrable, and the Allies agreed that the machine was a masterpiece in comparison with any immediate postwar helicopters. The stripped frame of this sole example is held in store at Coventry by the Midland Aircraft Preservation Society.

Flettner Fl 282B, c/n 28368, at the College of Technology, Cranfield. (*Foote PF(A) 268/7*)

Flugtechnische Fertigungsgemeinschaft

Prag FGP 227

BQ-UZ. This 1 : 3·75-scale wooden flying model of the Blohm und Voss Bv 238 six-engined flying-boat was built in Czechoslovakia, and was powered by six 21 hp ILO F 12/400 two-stroke air-cooled engines. It was first flown at Travemünde in September 1944 and after capture shipped to the MAEE Felixstowe for examination, where it was later broken-up.

Focke Achgelis

Fa 223 V14 Drache (Kite)

Built at Laupheim, near Stuttgart, this particular example, first flown in July 1943, was operated by Luft-Transportstaffel 40 from Ainring, Upper Austria, where it was captured by American troops in May 1945. Using its Versuch number, 14, as an identification, it was subsequently flown to the Airborne Forces Experimental Establishment, RAF Beaulieu, in September 1945, by the Luftwaffe crew, H. Gersenhauer (pilot), H. Zelewski (engineer) and F. Will (mechanic). It thus became the first helicopter to fly across the English Channel. Although intended for evaluation, in October 1945 it was destroyed after completing a total of 170 flying hours, before its characteristics could be established, when there was a failure of an auxiliary drive during the third test flight in the United Kingdom. As the failure occurred in a vertical ascent at approximately 60 feet from the ground, it was impossible to obtain the forward speed necessary for an autorotative landing, and the aircraft was completely wrecked.

Focke Achgelis Fa 223 V14 at the Airborne Forces Experimental Establishment, Beaulieu, in 1945.

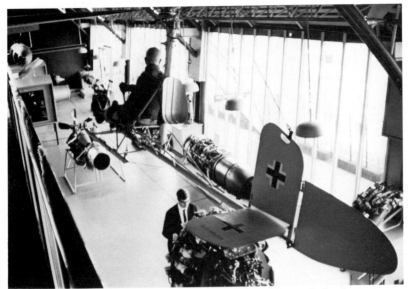

Focke Achgelis Fa 330, c/n 100509, at the Science Museum in London.

Fa 330 Bachsteltze (Water Wagtail)

At least eight examples of this single-seat autorotative kite, manufactured by Weser Flugzeugbau at Hoykenkamp, near Bremen, were shipped to the United Kingdom in about 1945. They had c/ns 100032, 100143, 100406, 100502, 100503, 100509, 100545 and 100549. Normally towed, and

Focke Achgelis Fa 330, c/n 100549, at Blackbushe in 1967. The rotor blades are missing.

therefore flown, from a submarine deck by a steel cable, working from a winch, some were tested, towed by a lorry, at the Airborne Forces Experimental Establishment, R.A.F. Beaulieu. Being one of the smallest, and therefore easiest, of ex-enemy aircraft to store and display, the majority are extant at various locations.

Focke-Wulf Fw 58 Weihe TE-BK at the RAE on 20 February, 1946. (*RAE*)

Focke-Wulf

Fw 58 Weihe (Kite)

TE-BK, of Fliegerforstschutzverband, later EKdo 40. Captured at Fassberg and ferried to the RAE, it was at Farnborough from 27 September, 1945, to 20 February, 1946, and was at one time at No. 6 MU Brize Norton. This Weihe was fitted with crop-dusting apparatus which included two venturi-shaped spray tubes under the forward fuselage. Development work for the modification of these spraying aircraft was undertaken by Vegesack Flugzeug Werke, near Bremen, about 30 aircraft being so modified. This aircraft was allotted Air Ministry number 117, but it is doubtful whether this was ever carried.

Fw 58 Weihe

During about 1945–46, Weihes with c/ns 2023, 2093, 2750, 2778, 2963, 3550, 3590, 58046 and 58348 were in RAF service, presumably as communications aircraft. Of these c/n 2093 was at the RAE on 26 January, 1946. One, coded LO-WQ was at the RAE on 18 April, 1946, and an unidentified Weihe was allotted Air Ministry number 126.

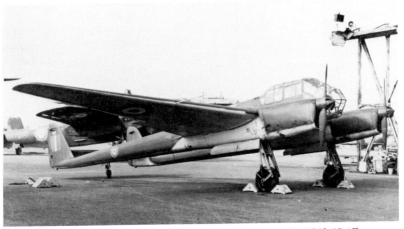

Focke-Wulf Fw 189A-3, c/n 0173, at the RAE in November 1945. (*RAE*)

Fw 189A-3 Uhu (Owl) (c/n 0173)

This twin-boom reconnaissance aircraft was at the RAE on 14 August, 1945, and put on exhibition that October and November. Allocated Air Ministry 27, it was flown to No. 6 MU Brize Norton for storage on 18 January, 1946. It was dark green overall with light blue undersurfaces.

Fw 190

The most advanced operational propeller-driven single-seat aircraft to serve with the Luftwaffe from 1941 to 1945. At least sixteen examples were examined and evaluated in the United Kingdom. Of the sixteen, only minimal information is available on the following:

A-3 sub-type, reputed to have served with No. 1426 (EAC) Flight, 1942–45, as MP498, although this serial was not officially allotted.

Two aircraft, sub-types unknown, which were allotted serials NF754 and NF755, and which were captured in the Middle East. They arrived in packing cases at RAF Collyweston on 12 December, 1943, and were subsequently flown by No. 1426 (EAC) Flight until transferred to the

Enemy Aircraft Flight, Central Fighter Establishment, RAF Tangmere, on 31 January, 1945. They were taken to No. 47 MU Sealand in November 1945 for storage and/or shipment.

A-3 sub-type, reputed to have been with the Air Fighting Development Unit, Duxford, in about 1942, as PM173, although this serial was not officially allotted.

C/n 180032 or 180082, sub-type unknown, was at the Enemy Aircraft Flight, Central Fighter Establishment, RAF Tangmere, in June 1945, in a wrecked condition.

C/n 733759, sub-type unknown, was at the RAE in about 1945–46.

In about 1945–46 Air Ministry numbers 11 and 230 were allocated to two Fw 190s, but it is not known to which specific airframes these numbers were applicable, although the former was later allotted to Ta 152H-1 (c/n 150168).

Fw 190A-3 (c/n 313)

British Intelligence was anxious to obtain an example of the Fw 190, and planned to mount a Commando raid (Operation Airthief) on an aerodrome in the Cherbourg peninsula in order to secure one. The raid was to have taken place in July 1942 and Supermarine test pilot Jeffrey Quill had been chosen to fly the captured Fw 190 back to Britain. But this operation was forestalled by the unexpected arrival of an intact BMW 801D-2 powered Fw 190A-3 on 23 June, 1942.

The Fw 190 which arrived in England carried the single chevron insignia of a Gruppen-Adjutant forward of the national markings and aft of them the vertical bar of III Gruppe. It was flown by Oberleutnant Arnim Faber, adjutant of III/JG2 whose Staffel, 7/JG2, was based at Morlaix.

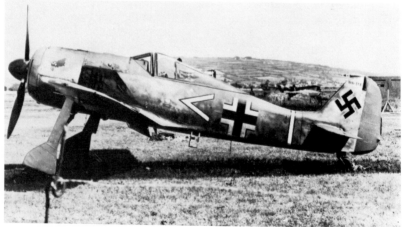

Focke-Wulf Fw 190A-3, c/n 313, at RAF Pembrey, with III/JG2's Cock's Head emblem on the engine cowling. (*IWM MH4190*)

Focke-Wulf Fw 190A-3, c/n 313, as MP499, with the AFDU, Duxford. (*IWM CH6411*)

On the evening of 23 June, 1942, the aircraft was engaged in a fight with Spitfires from the Exeter and Portreath Wings, which had previously attacked JG2's base, and after shooting down a Spitfire, Faber became disorientated, mistook the Bristol Channel for the English Channel, and, after making victory rolls across the aerodrome and extending the undercarriage while inverted, landed off a steep turn at RAF Pembrey.

The Fw 190 was taken by road to the RAE and, as MP499, was test flown on 3 July, 1942, by Wing Cmdr H. J. Wilson. Performance tests involved a total of nine hours' flying and, although formally transferred to the AFDU, Duxford, on 13 July, the aircraft was retained by the RAE for demonstration to interested visitors. The pilots were Wing Cmdr Campbell-Orde, OC AFDU, and Wing Cmdr Rankin, Biggin Hill.

On 22 July MP499 was flown in mock combat with a Spitfire IX, a Typhoon and Griffon Spitfire DP845, before representatives of the aircraft industry. A further extensive programme of trials with contemporary Allied fighters was flown at the AFDU—these included Mustang I AG349, a Spitfire IX and a Lockheed P-38 Lightning. The last recorded flight of MP499 was made by Flt Lt Robertson on 29 January, 1943. The aircraft was struck off charge on 18 September, 1943, the airframe being used for firing trials and the engine for bench tests.

While flown in Britain the aircraft had dark green and dark earth upper surfaces and yellow undersurfaces. A yellow prototype P was carried at one period.

Fw 190A-4 (c/n 171747)

This aircraft was on-charge at the Enemy Aircraft Flight, Central Fighter Establishment, Tangmere, in about June 1945, finished in a grey mottled scheme on the upper surfaces, with plain grey undersurfaces. At that time it carried the EAF identification EA-4. It was displayed at the RAE in October/November 1945.

Focke-Wulf Fw 190A-4/U8 PN999 at RAF Collyweston in November 1943.

Fw 190A-4/U8 (c/n 5843)

Red 9 of I/SKG 10. In the early hours of 20 May, 1943, Unteroffizier Heinz Ehrhardt was flying a night Jabo (fighter-bomber) operation to London and after crossing the English coast he received several vectors from base but nevertheless became lost. When his fuel began to run low he turned for home and, mistaking the north coast of Kent for the French coast, he eventually made a wheels-down landing at what he thought was St Omer but was in fact RAF Manston.

The aircraft was examined at the RAE, allotted serial PN999, and flown to the A & AEE, Boscombe Down, on 29 June, 1943, returning a month later. No. 1426 (EAC) Flight collected PN999 from the RAE on 28 September, and it was transferred to the Enemy Aircraft Flight, Central Fighter Establishment, Tangmere, on 31 January, 1945. PN999 was last flown, from the RAE to No. 6 MU Brize Norton, on 18 October, 1945, passing to No. 47 MU Sealand for storage on 1 November. PN999 had standard RAF dark green and dark earth upper surfaces and yellow undersurfaces.

Fw 190A-4/U8 (c/n 7155)

This aircraft belonged to II/SKG 10 and, except for the engine cowling, was painted a sooty matt black overall. It bore a yellow H aft of the Balkan cross and just discernible forward was a black equilateral triangle. This Focke-Wulf was one of a number of I and II Gruppen aircraft of SKG 10 which were sent out at midnight on 16 April, 1943, on the first experimental moonlight fighter-bomber attacks against southern England, the selected target being installations along the Thames near the Isle of Dogs in

Focke-Wulf Fw 190A4/U8, c/n 7155, shortly after landing at RAF West Malling in April 1943. (*IWM CH18222*)

Focke-Wulf Fw 190A-4/U8, c/n 7155, after being allocated serial PE882 but painted as E882.

Focke-Wulf Fw 190A-4/U8 PE882 at RNAS Yeovilton in about 1943.

London's East End. Flown by Feldwebel Otto Bechtold, the Fw 190 left the Amiens area with one 250 kg bomb and two drop-tanks carrying a total of 300 litres of fuel. The aircraft was put on a northerly heading over Cap Gris Nez and the drop tanks were jettisoned before crossing the Kent coast.

Navigation was difficult because of ground mist and Bechtold became lost. After flying on a northerly course for 40 minutes his aircraft was picked up by searchlights. He released the bomb and, after evading the searchlights, reduced height and headed back towards France. After about half an hour the pilot saw several searchlights pointing in the same direction and, the anti-aircraft fire having ceased, he thought he was over France. His fuel was running low so he followed the direction of the searchlights and saw the lights of an aerodrome. He lowered the undercarriage and landed at 01.10 to find himself at RAF West Malling.

The Fw 190 was flown to the RAE, given the serial PE882 and first flown with that identity on 20 April, 1943. It was delivered to No. 1426 (EAC) Flight at Collyweston on 23 April, 1944, but on 13 October crashed on the Stamford to Kettering road. The aircraft was seen to be on fire as it crashed through three walls and came to rest in the garden of a house. The pilot, Flt Lt E. R. Lewendon (Commanding Officer of No. 1426 Flight), was killed and the aircraft burnt out. At the time of the crash the Fw 190 was finished in standard RAF dark green and dark earth with yellow undersurfaces and had a yellow prototype P ahead of the fuselage roundel.

Fw 190A-5/U8 (c/n 2596)

White 6 of I/SKG 10. This aircraft took-off at 02.00 on 20 June, 1943, for a fighter-bomber operation in the London area, piloted by Unteroffizier Werner Ohne and carrying one 250 kg bomb and two drop-tanks. The weather forecast for this flight proved to be incorrect and considerable low cloud was encountered, in addition the R/T became unserviceable, and in consequence Ohne became lost. He turned south and after a while arrived over an airfield which he thought must be his own base as, by chance, the visual beacon was flashing the same characteristic. Thus it was he made a wheels-down landing at RAF Manston.

The aircraft was first flown by the RAE on 2 July and later used on performance and FuG 16Z radio equipment trials. It was delivered to the Air Fighting Development Unit, Wittering on 17 July, 1943, for tactical trials but during take-off on 25 June, 1944, the cockpit filled with smoke. The pilot made a forced landing but being blinded by the smoke bumped the aircraft's tail heavily causing serious kinking in the fuselage. The aircraft, at that time bearing serial PM679, was struck off charge and, on 11 July, delivered to No. 1426 (EAC) Flight, Collyweston, as a source of spares for PN999.

Fw 190A-6/R6 (c/n 550214)

This aircraft, reported to have been built by Bavart Flugzeugwerke, was displayed in Hyde Park, London, for Battle of Britain week in September 1945. It was allocated Air Ministry number 10 and, on 1 May, 1946, sent to No. 47 MU Sealand for crating. It was shipped to Cape Town on the ss *Perthshire*, arriving on 6 November, 1946, and is now in the Saxonwold Museum, Johannesburg.

Focke-Wulf Fw 190A-8, c/n 347763, at Boxted, Essex, in May 1945, with broad white or pale blue band around the engine cowling.

Fw 190A-8 (c/n 347763)

Captured by the USAAF and flown from Europe to Boxted, Essex, in May 1945. The BMW 801D-2 ran for about ten hours before eventually seizing, due to sand in the oil supply.

Fw 190A-8/R6 (c/n 733682)

Flown from Schleswig-Holstein to the RAE on 18 September, 1945, and subsequently exhibited, as the top component of the RAE mock-up Mistel in November 1945. Allocated Air Ministry number 75 and flown to No. 6 MU Brize Norton, for storage, on 30 November, 1945. Subsequently exhibited at various locations and now preserved at the Imperial War Museum.

Focke-Wulf Fw 190A-8/R6, c/n 733682, at Biggin Hill on 15 July, 1961.

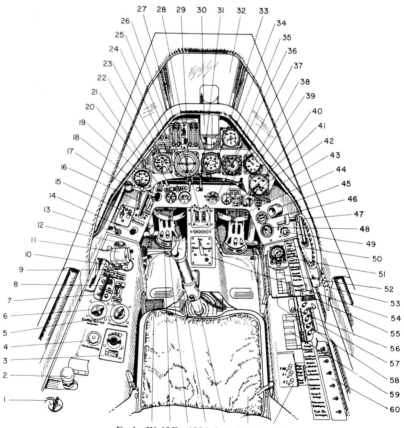

Focke-Wulf Fw 190A-8 cockpit layout.

Focke-Wulf Fw 190A-8/R6 c/n 733682, at the Imperial War Museum, London.

Fw 190D-9 (c/n 210079)

This example of the Jumo 213A-1 powered Fw 190 was Black 12 of 10/JG54. According to a Field Intelligence Report it bore the manufacturer's code NCC. Flown by Leutnant Theo Nibel, this aircraft took-off from Vorden to take part in Operation Bodenplatte—the large-scale attack on Allied aerodromes—on New Year's Day 1945. After attacking Grimbergen aerodrome, near Brussels, the coolant radiator was holed when the aircraft hit a partridge, and Nibel was forced to land at Wemmel to the northeast of the city. The aircraft suffered only slight damage and was exhibited at the RAE in October/November before being shipped to the United States where it received Foreign Equipment number FE-118.

In Luftwaffe service this Fw 190 was dark green on the upper fuselage with RLM (German Air Ministry) grey over light blue on the fuselage sides and undersurfaces. Upper surfaces of the wings had light and dark green splinter pattern camouflage. The spinner had a black and white spiral pattern, and the black 12 identification number was outlined in white.

Fw 190D-9 (c/n 210596)

This aircraft was at the RAE in about 1946. Its metal surfaces were thinly sprayed with dark green except for the undersurfaces which were pale blue-grey. Air Ministry number 77 was allocated but it is doubtful if it was actually carried, having previously been allotted to Ju 88A-6 c/n 2492. This Fw 190 went to No. 47 MU Sealand for crating and was among the German aircraft sent to South Africa on the ss *Perthshire* in October 1946. The aircraft finished up as scrap at a school at Benoni in the Transvaal.

A Focke-Wulf Fw 190F-8/U2 or U3, formerly of III/KG200, at the RAE in November 1945. (*RAE*)

Fw 190F-8/U2 or U3

Operated, at one time, by III/KG200, this aircraft was flown to the United Kingdom arriving at the RAE on 28 July, 1945. It was allocated Air Ministry 111 and flown from No. 6 MU Brize Norton to the RAE on 15 October, 1945, for the October/November exhibition. It was in storage or on exhibition at the College of Aeronautics, Cranfield, as late as 1948. The colour scheme was mottled dark blue, dark brown and dark green on the top surfaces, with light blue undersurfaces.

Focke-Wulf Fw 190S-8, c/n 584219, Air Ministry 29.

Fw 190S-8 (c/n 584219)

This was a conversion of an Fw 190A-8/F-8 and bore the code letters HRZ, either those of the manufacturer or a maintenance unit. It was at one time used by Jagdfliegerschule 103. The aircraft was flown from Schleswig to the RAE on 2 September, 1945, and allotted Air Ministry number 29. Subsequently, it was reported to have been allocated serial PN799 although this had originally been allotted to a Warwick GR.V. The Fw 190S-8 was flown to No. 6 MU Brize Norton on 5 September, and finally to No. 76 MU Wroughton, for crating, in July 1946. The aircraft was exhibited at various places and in 1976 was at RAF St Athan. It is the only remaining example of the two-seat trainer/liaison Fw 190. For some unknown reason it now bears the number 38.

Fw 200A-02 Condor (c/n 2894)

This was not a Luftwaffe aircraft, but the civil transport built at Bremen in 1938 and delivered to DDL, Danish Air Lines, on 14 July, 1938, as OY-DAM *Dania*. It arrived at Shoreham, near Brighton, on a scheduled service from Copenhagen on 8 April, 1940, and was seized the next day when Germany invaded Denmark.

It was given the British registration G-AGAY and named *Wolf* and then, on 9 January, 1941, officially impressed as DX177. On 12 July, during a test flight at White Waltham, it landed too fast and skidded on the wet grass, hitting a grass-cutting machine and a defence trench which caused the undercarriage to collapse. The aircraft was not repaired and was written off as scrap on 18 January, 1942.

DDL's other Condor, OY-DEM *Jutlandia* (c/n 2993), was damaged landing at Northolt in 1946. It was dismantled there the following year.

Focke-Wulf Fw 200A-02, c/n 2894, OY-DAM *Dania* of DDL—Danish Air Lines. (*SAS-DDL*)

Focke-Wulf Fw 200C-4/U1 Air Ministry 94 at the RAE in November 1945. The circular Staffel emblem, enclosing a bird's head, was carried on both sides of the nose. (*RAE*)

Fw 200C-4/U1 Condor (c/n 0137)

Originally CE-IB and later GC-AE of Regierungs-Staffel, with ground handling number 5 on the rudder. Found intact at Achmer in 1945 and exhibited at the RAE in October/November with Air Ministry number 94. This example was used by Heinrich Himmler as a personal transport, and was an adaptation of the Atlantic commerce raider, mounting guns in upper and lower turrets, and having accommodation for 11 passengers. Himmler's seat, in his private compartment, faced forward on the starboard side and was armour-plated. An additional movable sheet of armour-plate was hinged on the side of the seat, and in one position, bolted to the side of the seat, the armour formed protection against bullets fired in a beam attack, and when allowed to fall back it guarded against stray bullets from tail attacks. Opposite the seat was an airspeed indicator and an altimeter. There was also a personal escape window. The finish was splinter pattern green camouflage on the top surfaces, with light blue undersurfaces and yellow lower engine cowlings.

Fw 200C-4 Condor

At one time with the Regierungs-Staffel, with ground handling number 9 on the rudder. Found intact at Achmer and was at the RAE in about 1945 with Air Ministry number 95. The finish was the same as on Himmler's aircraft.

Two further Fw 200C-4s were in the United Kingdom in about 1945, with Air Ministry numbers 96 and 97. No further details are available.

Focke-Wulf Ta 152H-0, c/n 150003, Red 4. (*IWM HU2920*)

Ta 152H-0 (c/n 150003)

Built at Cottbus and bearing Red 4, this example was captured at Langenhagen. It was test flown by the RAF in 1945 and, later, by the RAE. It was shipped to the United States, becoming FE-112, and stored for the Smithsonian Institution.

Ta 152H-1 (c/n 150168)

Also built at Cottbus, this aircraft was 9 of Stabs-Schwarm/JG301. It was flown to the RAE in an Arado Ar 232B-0 and subsequently flown to No. 6 MU Brize Norton. After an air test by Lt-Cmdr E. M. Brown on 18 August, 1945, it was returned to the RAE for the October/November exhibition. It was allotted Air Ministry number 11 although this had previously been given to an Fw 190. This Ta 152 had green upper surfaces, grey-green side surfaces aft, light blue undersurfaces and red spinner with white spiral.

Focke-Wulf Ta 152H-1, c/n 150168, at the RAE. Traces of the figure 9 can be seen beneath the rear of the cockpit canopy and the Reichsverteidigung (Defence of the Reich) fuselage band is visible. (*IWM HU2395*)

Gotha Go 145B, c/n 1115, SM-NQ just after its arrival at Lewes racecourse on 28 August, 1940.

Gotha

Go 145B (c/n 1115)

Powered by an Argus III, this advanced trainer, SM-NQ of Stab/JG27 was based at Cherbourg-Ouest. On 28 August, 1940, flown by Leonard Buckle, it was being used to fly mail to Strasbourg when the pilot lost his way. Running short of fuel he landed on Lewes racecourse. Still in Luftwaffe markings it was flown to the RAE by Sq Ldr H. J. Wilson on 31 August. With RAF markings and the serial BV207 it was flight tested on 12 December, and on 1 January, 1941, was flown to No. 20 MU Aston Down. It went to Maintenance Command in September 1941 as 2682M.

Gotha Go 145B, c/n 1115, after its acquisition by the RAF but before the application of the serial BV207.

Go 150

An example of this twin-engined two-seat light aircraft was used by the Station CO, at RAF Kenley, probably in 1946–47. It was blue overall.

Heinkel He 59B-2 D-ASUO was white overall with red crosses, black registration and grey Luftwaffe eagle.

Heinkel

He 59B-2

Carrying the civil registration D-ASUO, in addition to Red Cross markings on the nose and under the wingtips, this twin-float biplane of Seenotflugkommando 1 was based at Boulogne. On 9 July, 1940, with Unteroffizier Helmut Bartmann (pilot), Unteroffizier Walter Anders (observer), Unteroffizier Erich Schiele (wireless operator) and Feldwebel Gunther Maywald (flight engineer), it took-off from Boulogne to fly via Calais to the Ramsgate area to look for the pilot of a Bf 109, said to have been shot down over the Channel earlier in the day. It was subsequently attacked by Spitfires, although unarmed, and was credited to Pilot Officer J. L. Allen of No. 54 Squadron when it alighted intact on the Goodwin Sands, off Ramsgate, at 20.00 hr. Apart from a broken petrol feed pipe to the tank, it suffered no damage and was towed ashore by the Walmer lifeboat and beached near the lifeboat station. Although scheduled for evaluation by the MAEE it is believed to have been broken-up *in situ*, no doubt souvenir hunters contributed to this!

Heinkel He 111H-1 AW177, c/n 6853, at the RAE. (*RAE*)

He 111H-1 (c/n 6853)

This medium bomber was built at Heinkel's Oranienburg factory and delivered, on 22 August, 1939, as 1H-EN of 5/KG26 based at Westerland, Sylt. Although it has been reported as having c/n 6353, the c/n 6853 appeared in the bomb-bay compartment.

On 9 February, 1940, this aircraft took-off on a mission to attack shipping in the Firth of Forth. The crew comprised Unteroffiziers Helmut Meyer (pilot), Franz Wieners (wireless operator), Josef Sangel (observer), and Obergefreiter Heinz Hedgemann (bomb-aimer/gunner). While *en route* it was attacked by Spitfire I, K9962, flown by Sq Ldr A. D. Farquhar of No. 602 Squadron, and was forced-down on moorland near Berwick Law, the wireless operator being killed in the action. Although it collided with a low stone wall the damage, which included punctured oil tanks, was minimal, and the aircraft was repaired on site and moved to RAF Turnhouse, from where it was flown to the RAE, via Finningley, on 14 August, escorted by two Hurricanes. Allotted serial AW177, it was transferred to the Air Fighting Development Unit, Duxford, on 12 September, 1941, returning to the RAE on 6 October, being transferred to No. 1426 (EAC) Flight, Duxford, on 7 December. It was operated by that unit for nearly two years, but on 10 November, 1943, while landing at Polebrook, AW177 and the Ju 88A-5 HM509 used the same runway from opposite ends. The pilot of the Heinkel, Flying Officer F. A. 'Freddy' Barr, opened up the engines and did a steep turn to port, stalled, and spun-in vertically just outside the airfield perimeter. In addition to Barr, six of the ten passengers on board were killed when the fuel tanks exploded on impact. Flt Lt Forbes and Flying Officer Lewendon entered the blazing cockpit area to rescue survivors, subsequently receiving a commendation from the USAAF Station Commander. The aircraft's colour at this time was dark green and dark earth upper surfaces, yellow undersurfaces and black propeller blades and spinners.

Heinkel He 111H-1, c/n 6853, carried the badge of the Löwen (Lion) Kampfgeschwader, KG-26, on both sides of the fuselage, forward of the wing leading edge. This was retained while in British markings. (*Flight International 17996S*)

Heinkel He 111H-1, c/n 6853. View of the bomb-bay compartment looking aft. The constructor's number can be seen. (*Flight International 17999S*)

Heinkel He 111H-23, c/n 701152, at Tangmere in about 1945.

He 111H-23 (c/n 701152)

Captured by the USAAF and subsequently on-charge at the Enemy Aircraft Flight, Central Fighter Establishment, Tangmere, the aircraft was exhibited at the RAE in October and November 1945 in combined Luftwaffe, USAAF and RAF markings. Its basic colouring was black overall with red rudder, a small swastika in a diamond shaped badge on the fin, RAF roundel and USAAF bar on the fuselage and USAAF star and bar under the starboard wing. Ahead of the roundel, in red outlined in white, were the code letters HV, and aft was a concentric motif, in the same colours, consisting of the letters OCW. Over the radio operator's position were the radio call code letters NT-FL. This He 111 was subsequently placed in storage at RAF Fulbeck, and was later exhibited at various locations, at one time coded CW-HV. In 1976 it was at RAF St Athan.

Heinkel He 111H-23, c/n 701152, at St Athan.

He 111

There was one He 111 which did not become captive. At 23.00 hr on 14 February, 1941, it was landed at RAF Debden and taxied to the control tower but, realising their error, the crew took-off again, and it could have been this aircraft which visited two other RAF stations on the night of 14–15 February.

He 115

Some He 115 twin-engined twin-float reconnaissance and anti-shipping seaplanes were operated by the Norwegian Marinens Flyvevapen and when Germany invaded Norway on 9 April, 1940, an He 115A-2 of No. 2 Flyavdeling was flown to the MAEE at Helensburgh. When hostilities ended in June four more He 115s set out for the United Kingdom. These were three He 115A-2s of No. 3 Flyavdeling and a Luftwaffe He 115B-1 of 1/Küstenfliegergruppe 506 which had been captured by the Norwegians.

An ex-Norwegian Marinens Flyvevapen Heinkel He 115 in RAF markings. (*IWM E(MOS) 1230*)

Three reached Sullom Voe in Shetland but one ran out of fuel and had to be sunk after its forced alighting. The survivors were sent to Helensburgh to join the first.

The He 115s retained their Norwegian markings until February 1941 when they were overhauled by Scottish Aviation and given RAF markings. The He 115A-2s became BV184 (ex-56 of NMF), BV185 (ex-58) and BV186 (ex-62), and the He 115B-1 became BV187 (ex-64).

BV184 went to BOAC at Hythe on Southampton Water in May 1941 and, as an experimental aircraft, to Calshot in June. It flew from Calshot to

Land's End and back on fuel consumption trials on 23 April, 1942, was transferred to Wig Bay the following month, and struck off charge on 31 May after catching fire while being refuelled.

BV185 also went to BOAC at Hythe in May 1941 and to Calshot that June. Later it was modified for clandestine operations. Much of the glazed panelling of the cockpit enclosures was removed and the defensive armament was increased by the installation of eight 0·303-in Browning guns in the wings—four firing aft. It was flown to Mountbatten on 27 October, 1941, and then to Malta by Lieut Haakon Offerdahl. Painted with Luftwaffe markings, BV185 began operation by alighting in daylight in Tripoli harbour to pick up two Allied agents who were then flown to Malta. The aircraft was struck off charge on 1 April, 1942, having been destroyed when its hangar received a direct hit during a German air attack.

BV186 went to BOAC at Hythe in May 1941 and to Stranraer in July 1942. Its subsequent history is not known, although it was modified for clandestine operations and was photographed on 1 October, 1942, when it was still intact.

BV187 went to BOAC at Hythe in May 1941 and, as an experimental aircraft, to Calshot that June. It was modified for clandestine operations and based at RAF Woodhaven on the south bank of the Tay near Dundee. It was operated on flights to Norway, flown by Lieut K. Skavhaugen, but the risks were too great and the operations with the He 115 abandoned. The aircraft is believed to have been broken up on the Tay late in 1943. When based in Scotland this aircraft had blue and grey upper surfaces and black undersurfaces.

He 115 (c/n 2754)

8L-GH of 1/Küstenfliegergruppe 906. This example, crewed by Leutnant z.S. Otto Aldus, Hauptmann Heinrich Kothe and Unteroffizier Meissner, landed in a field at Rosehearty, near Fraserburgh in Aberdeenshire on 17 September, 1940, during a mine-laying mission, the pilot admitting he thought he was over the Firth of Tay! It was subsequently removed to the MAEE Helensburgh.

He 162 Salamander

At least eleven examples of the diminutive Volksjager (People's Fighter) were captured at Leck, Schleswig-Holstein, by British forces and subsequently airlifted to the United Kingdom in captured Ar 232B transports. The fighters had originally been issued to I/Jagdgeschwader 1 at Parchim in March 1945 but no fully authenticated reports of operational usage have come to light. One Staffelkapitän had marked 16 victory-bars on the fin of his aircraft but these victories had in fact been obtained on types he had previously flown.

Heinkel He 162A, c/n 120235, at the Imperial War Museum, London.

He 162A (c/n 120021 or 120221)

Allocated Air Ministry 58 and serial VH526, it was operated by the RAE Aerodynamics Flight in about 1945 and eventually cannibalized to keep other examples airworthy.

He 162A (c/n 120235)

6 of 1/JG1. This aircraft was allocated Air Ministry 63 and fitted with British instrumentation. It is reported to have been test flown at the RAE, probably in 1945–46, and was subsequently in store at No. 6 MU Brize Norton. It is now in the Imperial War Museum, London, as 6 of JG77.

Heinkel He 162A Air Ministry 63, equipped with British instruments. (*IWM MH6972*)

Heinkel He 162A-2, c/n 120072, Air Ministry 61 at the RAE in 1945. (*RAE*)

He 162A-2 (c/n 120072)

With Air Ministry allocation 61, this aircraft was operated by the RAE Aerodynamics Flight in 1945. Four evaluation flights, totalling 50 minutes, were made but on the last of these, on 9 November, 1945, the aircraft crashed and was destroyed. During a low-level roll one fin and rudder collapsed, after which the tail unit broke away and the aircraft fell into the Oudenarde Barracks at Aldershot. The pilot, Flt Lt R. A. Marks, was unable to abandon the aircraft and was killed.

He 162A-2 (c/n 120074)

Allocated Air Ministry 60, this aircraft was White 11 of 3/JG1. It was flown by Staffelkapitän Oberleutnant Erich Demuth and he had 16 victory bars painted on the aircraft although his victories had been scored on other types of aircraft. The number 20 appeared in small white numerals above and behind the main code number. This He 162 was in store at No. 6 MU Brize Norton in March 1946.

He 162A-2 (c/n 120076)

Allocated Air Ministry 59 and serial VH523, this aircraft was flown for a total of 1½ hours by the RAE before being shipped to Canada. This He 162 is still in existence at Rockcliffe, Ontario.

Heinkel He 162A-2, c/n 120086, Air Ministry 62 in Hyde Park in September 1945.

He 162A-2 (c/n 120086)

2 of 2/JG1. This example, Air Ministry 62, was exhibited in Hyde Park, London, during Battle of Britain week in September 1945. It was in store at No. 6 MU Brize Norton in March 1946 and later that year was shipped to Canada. It is now at Rockcliffe, Ontario. This aircraft had dark green upper surfaces and medium grey undersurfaces which extended half way up the fuselage. The medium grey was carried over the top of the nose, and the fins and rudders were light grey.

He 162A-2 (c/n 120091)

Little is known about this aircraft except that it was allocated Air Ministry number 66 and displayed at the RAE Farnborough in October/November 1945.

He 162A-2 (c/n 120097)

This aircraft was 4 of 2/JG1 at the time of its capture but at some time had carried the number 3. It was allocated Air Ministry number 64 and serial VN153 and displayed at the RAE in October/November 1945.

He 162A-2 (c/n 120098)

Allocated Air Ministry number 67 and, unofficially, serial VH515, this aircraft was first flown by Lt-Cmdr E. M. Brown at the RAE on 7 September, 1945.

Heinkel He 162A-2, c/n 120223, at Leck, with personnel of No. 1426 (EAC) Flight in May or June 1945.

He 162A-2 (c/n 120223)

Although it is doubtful whether this example was sent to the United Kingdom, it is believed to have been allocated Air Ministry number 68.

He 162A-2 (c/n 120227)

Red 2 of 2/JG1. Allocated Air Ministry 65 and serial VH513, this aircraft was operated by the RAE Aerodynamics Flight and made 26 flights totalling 11 hr 45 min. At that time it had dark and olive green upper surfaces and pale blue-grey undersurfaces. The aircraft was in store at RAF Leconfield in about 1946 and was subsequently exhibited at various places, carrying the code numbers 27, 12 and Red 2 of JG77. This He 162 has been restored to its original condition and in 1976 was at RAF St Athan.

Heinkel He 162A-2, c/n 120227, Air Ministry 65, on a test flight at the RAE in about 1945.
(*Flight International 19002S*)

Heinkel He 162A-2, c/n 120227, at Colerne in 1969.

He 177A-5/R6 Greif (Griffon)

Two examples of this heavy bomber, which had justifiably earned the nickname of 'Flaming Coffin' because the Daimler-Benz DB 610As were prone to overheating and therefore a fire hazard, were acquired for test and evaluation in the United Kingdom. The first, captured by French Resistance forces at Blagnac, near Toulouse, in September 1944, is reported to have had the c/n 412951, but readers are referred to the Bf 109G-6/U2, TP814, for evidence to the contrary. Its original Luftwaffe camouflage was a splinter pattern of black- green and dark green on the top surfaces, and pale blue with large irregular patches of light grey on the undersurfaces. The aircraft was flown to the RAE by Wing Commander 'Roly' Falk, with Sq Ldr Pearse as engineer, on 10 September, 1944, in a flight time of 2 hr 45 min. AAEF black and white stripes were painted over the Luftwaffe camouflage. It bore French red, white and pale blue rudder stripes which were later over-painted red, and an RAF red, white and blue fin flash was added on arrival in Britain. Additionally, RAF roundels were painted over the previous French type, the serial TS439 and a yellow

Heinkel He 177A-5/R6 at the RAE just after arrival on 10 September, 1944, but before the addition of RAF roundels, fin flash and serial TS439. (*RAE*)

55

prototype P being added; but the code F8 of II/KG40, based at Bordeaux (Merignac), and the French inscription *Prise de Guerre*, were retained. It was flown, as TS439, for the first time on 20 September, 1944, on spring-tab tests, and subsequently made about twelve flights from the RAE, landing at the A & AEE, Boscombe Down, after a 'bombing-run', on 20 February, 1945. It is reported to have been shipped to the United States in April 1945, but the A & AEE believe it was broken-up.

The other example, from the same unit, II/KG40, was ferried from Villacoublay to the RAE on 14 January, 1945, by Flt Lt Randrup, but after one handling flight it was delivered to the USAAF at Bovingdon on 19 January, and is believed to have been shipped to the United States. It may have been unofficially allotted the serial TS478.

He 219 Uhu (Owl)

One of, if not the, finest night fighters produced in Germany during the Second World War. Five examples were flown from Schleswig to the RAE, four A-2s, and a single A-5/R2 which had been the V11 pre-production airframe. They were possibly all at one time with I/NJG1.

C/n 310189 was the V11 airframe modified to A-5/R2 standard, being ferried from Schleswig to the RAE on 27 August, 1945, and allotted Air Ministry number 22. It was painted light grey overall with two shades of grey mottling on the top surfaces. There were traces of the overpainted code CL on the aft fuselage, and V1 on the nose. It was operated by the Enemy Aircraft Flight, Central Fighter Establishment, Tangmere, on comparative radar trials during September 1945, and was exhibited at the RAE in October/November. It was still in storage at No. 6 MU Brize Norton in July 1947.

C/n 290126, A-2, flown from the RAE to No. 6 MU Brize Norton on 21 August, 1945.

C/n 310106, A-2, flown from the Enemy Aircraft Flight, Central Fighter Establishment, Tangmere, to the RAE on 19 October, 1945.

C/n 310109, A-2, flown from the RAE to RAF Abingdon on 30 August, 1945, and to No. 6 MU Brize Norton the following day.

Heinkel He 219 V11 (A-5/R2), c/n 310189, at the RAE in November, 1945. (*RAE*)

Heinkel He 219A-2 at RNAS Ford in the summer of 1945. It is believed to have had c/n 310215. (*Newark Air Museum 5951*)

C/n 310215, A-2, was with the Enemy Aircraft Flight, Central Fighter Establishment, Tangmere, in about June 1945.

Air Ministry numbers 20, 21, 43 and 44 were allocated but it is not known to which aircraft the numbers applied. No. 20 was used for braking tests, and No. 21 was the last example to survive in the United Kingdom, being broken-up early in 1948.

Henschel

Hs 129B-1 (c/n 0397)

Only one example of this anti-tank and close support aircraft was evaluated in the United Kingdom. This aircraft had been operated in North Africa by 4/Sch G2 and it was shipped to the United Kingdom, arriving at No. 1426 (EAC) Flight, Collyweston, on 27 June, 1943. On arrival it was found that both wings had been damaged in combat and considerable repair and

Henschel Hs 129B-1 at RAF Collyweston on 15 February 1944. The aircraft is still in Luftwaffe camouflage, complete with white fuselage band. The starboard section of the fin and rudder, and undersurface of the starboard wing are missing.

reconstruction was necessary, the aircraft only being ready for flight on 2 September, 1944. On the following day, as NF756, it was flown by Flt Lt R. F. Forbes, but its Gnome-Rhône 14M engines gave persistent trouble and the aircraft was grounded on 8 November. It was transferred to the Enemy Aircraft Flight, Central Fighter Establishment, Tangmere, and then, on 1 November, 1945, put into store at No. 47 MU Sealand. It is known to have been at No. 6 MU Brize Norton in July 1947, at which time it had dark green and dark earth upper surfaces and yellow undersurfaces. When captured the aircraft bore a yellow C and should have been with the 3rd Staffel.

One of the few Henschel Hs 130s to be completed.

Hs 130A-0/U6

The front fuselage and pressure cabin of this twin-engined, two-seat, high-altitude reconnaissance aircraft was at RAF Kenley about 1945–47.

Horten

Ho IV (8-251) (c/n HAC 289)

Built at Königsberg (Neuhaus) in 1941, this single-seat high-performance tailless glider, with prone-pilot position, was exhibited at the RAE Farnborough in October/November 1945, still bearing its original code letters LA-AC. It was subsequently allotted serial number VP543 and test flown on a number of occasions. In May 1950 the Ho IV was given a Certificate of Airworthiness and the British Gliding Association number BGA 647. This glider later went to the United States and was registered N79289.

Horten Ho IV LA-AC at the RAE in November 1945. (*Flight International 190115*)

Ho IX (Gotha Go 229 V3)

This twin-jet tailless single-seat fighter was under development by Gothaer Waggonfabrik at Friedrichsrode where it was found abandoned by the VIII Corps of the United States Third Army on 14 April, 1945. When discovered, the unfinished aircraft was standing on its own nosewheel undercarriage but the outer wings had not been fitted. The aircraft was sent to the RAE and re-assembled and consideration was given to its completion, the fitting of British engines and flight testing, but this was not done and the aircraft was sent to the United States where it received Foreign Equipment number FE-490. When last heard of the Go 229 was in store for the Smithsonian Institution.

Junkers

Ju 52/3m

Numerous examples of this three-engined corrugated-metal skinned transport were captured and operated for communications and other purposes. The following serial numbers were allocated to aircraft of this type: VM892, VM900–932, VM961–987, VN176–7, VN709–731 and VN740–756. From these batches one was allocated to Railway Air Services and ten to British European Airways for domestic operations, all were of the g8e sub-type.

The Railway Air Services Ju 52/3m was VM908/G-AHBP (c/n 6750). It had been built at Dessau in 1939 and had been in service with Lufthansa as

Junkers Ju 52/3mg8e, c/n 501441, G-AHOC at Croydon in 1946.

D-APZX *Raoul Stoisvljevic*. With RAS it was based at Liverpool Airport (Speke). It was registered to BEA on 1 February, 1947, and scrapped at Castle Bromwich, Birmingham, in February 1948.

The BEA aircraft were: G-AHOC/VM923 (c/n 501441), G-AHOD/VN740 (c/n 131150), G-AHOE/VN723, G-AHOF/VN729, G-AHOG/VM979 (c/n 3317), G-AHOH/VN746 (c/n 641364), G-AHOI/VN744 (c/n 641227), G-AHOJ/VN756 (c/n 500138), G-AHOK/VN742 (c/n 2998) and G-AHOL/VN741 (c/n 641213).

These aircraft were introduced on the Croydon–Liverpool–Belfast route on 18 November, 1946, on some Scottish routes on 1 February, 1947, and on nonstop Croydon–Belfast services on 20 March, 1947. G-AHOK was damaged in a training accident at Renfrew, Glasgow, all were withdrawn at the end of August 1947, and they were broken up at Ringway, Manchester, early in 1948.

Junkers Ju 52/3mg11e, c/n 641038, Air Ministry 104 at the RAE in August 1945. It has dark green top surfaces with light blue undersurfaces. (*RAE*)

Fuselage of one of the captured Ju 52/3ms, in the Woodley area (1945–48) with original Luftwaffe camouflage scheme.

In addition there were a number of other Ju 52/3ms which saw some service. Three were allocated Air Ministry numbers 102, 103 and 104. Nothing is known about Air Ministry 102 except that it was scrapped in 1948. Air Ministry 103 was at No. 6 MU Brize Norton and flown from there to the RAE on 3 November, 1945, giving a flight demonstration on the following day and being flown back to Brize Norton on 14 November. It was scrapped in 1948. Air Ministry 104 (c/n 641038) had been Lufthansa's D-AUAV. It was taken over by the RAF at Flensburg on 4 May, 1945, and flown from Blankensee, near Lübeck, to the RAE by Sq Ldr Somerville on 18 July for use by the RAE's General Duties Flight.

Another Ju 52/3m, c/n 5375, is known to have been flown from Schleswig to Eggebeck on 14 June, 1945, by Flt Lt D. G. M. Gough and from Tangmere to Knokke and Schleswig on 18 June by Sq Ldr Somerville. This aircraft carried the RAE General Duties Flight identification GD1.

Two civil registered Ju 52/3ms, D-AGAC and D-AKUA (an ex-Lufthansa aircraft), are known to have been flown to No. 6 MU Brize Norton on 26 and 30 July, 1945, respectively, and D-AUAN and D-AUAU have been reported as being in the United Kingdom, but this cannot be confirmed.

Ju 52/3m (See)

Three examples of Ju 52/3m floatplanes were at the MAEE Felixstowe in 1945–46. They were painted black overall.

Ju 87B-1 (c/n 5167)

This dive-bomber, S2-JN of 5/St G77, crash-landed intact at Goring Hall golf course, near Ferring, on the afternoon of 18 August, 1940, after attacking Poling radar station in Sussex, one crew member, Oberfeldwebel Willy Geiger, being killed. Pilfering of vital parts prevented evaluation of the aircraft by the RAE and it was therefore burned where it had landed, although an undercarriage leg and wheel spat have been preserved. The upper surfaces were dark green, the undersurfaces light blue and the spinner yellow. The spat now carries a red J.

Ju 87B (c/n 1394?)

A5-DN of 5/St G1. This is believed to have been a Ju 87B-1. It was brought down reasonably intact in the Swanage area of Dorset on 8 August, 1940, and removed to the RAE for examination. The rear section of the fuselage, bearing a yellow D, still exists and was at Bournemouth in 1976.

Ju 87D-3/Trop (c/n 2883)

This version of the Ju 87 was captured in Europe and appears to have been partially converted, at some time, to Ju 87G configuration, having the original short-span wings, hard-points for anti-tank cannon, and no dive-brakes. Reported to have been allocated Air Ministry number 37, this aircraft was at the RAE in about 1945 and then taken to the Air Historical Branch's official store at RAF Fulbeck. It was exhibited at various places, with codes which included RI-JK, W8 and W8-A, and in 1976 was still at St Athan.

Junkers Ju 87D-3/Trop, c/n 2883, at RAF Henlow prior to its proposed use in the Battle of Britain film.

Ju 88

The Ju 88 was used as a bomber, dive-bomber, day and night fighter, minelayer, torpedo-dropper, intruder, operational trainer, photographic reconnaissance and ground attack aircraft, and more than 15,000 were built. It was one of the truly outstanding aircraft of the Second World War, and more that 30 examples were examined or evaluated in the United Kingdom. Only very little information has survived on some of these aircraft.

Ju 88A-1 (c/n 0362)

Built by the Nord-Deutsche Dornier Werke and operated by 4(F)/121, this aircraft bore the code 7A-FM in black outlined in white. At 14.00 on 19 September, 1940, it left Caen on a photographic and weather reconnaissance flight with a crew comprising Unteroffizier Hans-Jurgen Zscheket (pilot), Leutnant Helmuth Knab (observer), Unteroffizier Josef Thoring (wireless operator) and Obergefreiter Erich Bresch (gunner). They succeeded in taking their photographs but on their return flight the port engine developed a defect and the crew, having sighted Allied fighters in the vicinity, decided to make a wheels-up landing at RAF Oakington. The aircraft was taken to the RAE for examination.

Cockpit section of Ju 88A-1, c/n 0362, under examination at the RAE. The badge of 4(F)/121 comprised a black owl gripping a red pencil in its claws, on a white background outlined in red.
(IWM E(MOS) 135)

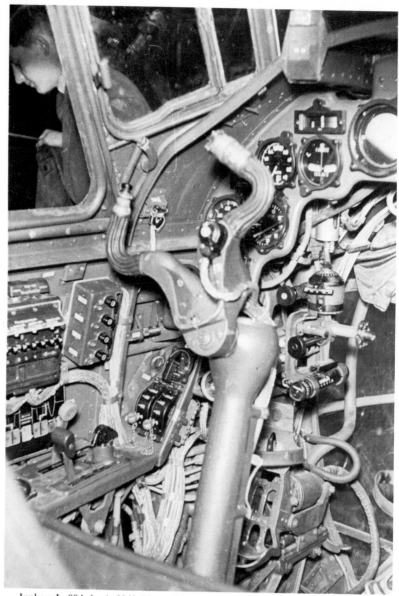

Junkers Ju 88A-1, c/n 0362. View of the port pilot's position. (*IWM E(MOS) 121*)

Junkers Ju 88A-1, c/n 7036, AX919 at the RAE in 1940 or 1941. It has dark green and dark earth top surfaces, with yellow undersurfaces. (*IWM MH4192*)

Ju 88A-1 (c/n 2142)

3Z-DK of 2/KG77, based at Laon. This aircraft, crewed by Oberleutnant Friedrich Oeser, Gefreiter Hulsmann, Oberfeldwebel Gorke and Unteroffizier Klasing, crash-landed on Gatwick racecourse at 17.00 on 30 September, 1940, Klasing being killed in the crash. The aircraft was taken to the RAE for examination and subsequently exhibited in Cambridgeshire and Hertfordshire.

Ju 88A-1 (c/n 7036)

9K-HL of 3/KG51. On 28 July, 1940, this Dessau-built Ju 88 with a crew of four—Oberfeldwebel Josef Bier (pilot), Leutnant Willi Ruckdeschel (observer), and Unteroffiziers Heinz Ohls (wireless operator) and Martin Multhammer (flight engineer)—was on a sortie over England when the direction-finding equipment failed and the crew lost their way. Being short

Junkers Ju 88A-1, c/n 7036, with the badge of the Edelweiss Kampfgeschwader, KG51, carried on both sides of the nose, beneath the front cockpit canopy. The badge was not retained when the aircraft flew as AX919. (*Flight International 17992S*)

of fuel a forced landing was made in a clover field at Buckholt Farm, just north of Bexhill. The Ju 88 was virtually undamaged and was taken on charge by the RAE as AX919 on 31 August. It was test flown on 3 April, 1941, and on a few other occasions, but on 12 June, 1942, it was taken by road to Duxford and No. 1426 (EAC) Flight used it as a source of spares for HM509, the Ju 88A-5 (c/n 6073).

Junkers Ju 88A-5 4D-DL (c/n 3457) at Broadfield Down on 24 July, 1941, the aerodrome being still under construction.

Ju 88A-5 (c/n 3457)

4D-DL of 3/KG30, with Staffel letter L in yellow. With a crew comprising Unteroffizier Wolfgang Hosie (pilot), Feldwebel Paul Zimmermann (observer), and Obergefreiters Franz Sander (wireless operator) and Robert Riemann (gunner), this aircraft took-off from Lanvéoc (Poulmic) in France at 23.35 on 23 July, 1941, to attack the docks at Birkenhead. The target was attacked after a flight west of the Scillies and over the Irish Sea at 6,000 ft. On the return flight the crew confused Beacon 173 at Audierne with a British radio beacon working on the same wavelength and with mist covering South Wales and Somerset and a balloon barrage in an appropriate position, the upper part of the Bristol Channel looked similar to the Brest Roads. The inexperienced Ju 88 crew believed they were over France and by mistake landed at RAF Broadfield Down, Wrington, near Bristol, at 06.20 on 24 July. The RAF station was then under construction, and later became Lulsgate Bottom.

With a Hurricane escort, Sq Ldr H. J. Wilson flew the Ju 88 from Broadfield Down to the RAE where it was taken on charge by A Flight on 1 August as EE205. On 14 August, in its new markings, it was flown to the A & AEE and back, and after tactical trials with the Air Fighting Development Unit, Duxford, in August, it remained at Farnborough until 28 August, 1942, when it was flown to No. 1426 (EAC) Flight at Duxford.

During fighter affiliation trials with No. 235 Squadron at Chivenor on 24 November, 1942, the turning radius of the Ju 88 led to the loss of Beaufighter IC T5253. The Beaufighter, chasing the Junkers, stalled in a tight turn and dived into the mud of the river Taw. In the official accident

Junkers Ju 88A-5, (c/n 3457) as EE205, preparing to take-off from RAF Hardwick, *en route* to RAF Bungay, on 12 March, 1943.

report it was stated "the pilot (of the Beaufighter) forgot that the Beaufighter's turn is wider than the German type". The Beaufighter disappeared into the mud, and it proved impossible to extract it or the crew.

On 31 January, 1945, EE205 transferred to the Enemy Aircraft Flight, Central Fighter Establishment, Tangmere, and that November went to No. 47 MU Sealand for storage.

Ju 88A-5 (c/n 6073)

M2-MK of Küstenfliegergruppe 106. This aircraft, with a crew comprising Unteroffizier Erwin Herms (pilot), Obergefreiter Ernst Kurz (observer), Gefreiter Heinrich Klein (wireless operator) and Obergefreiter Friedrich Krautler (gunner), left Morlaix at 16.00 on 26 November, 1941, to attack shipping which had been reported in the Irish Sea. It flew up the Irish Sea to a point between Bardsey Island and Wicklow but in spite of a prolonged search no shipping was sighted. Fuel then began to run low and Herms turned for home. Due to a miscalculation of the wind strength the crew

Junkers Ju 88A-5, c/n 6073, HM509 with early paint scheme and the original code M2-MK. It is seen at Duxford in 1942 before reverting to German markings for film production.

Junkers Ju 88A-5 HM509 still showing traces of the Luftwaffe code M2-MK. (*IWM E(MOS)1252A*)

mistook Cardigan for North Devon and Pembroke for Plymouth. The Ju 88 continued south and when it actually passed over Plymouth the crew thought they had reached the Bay of Biscay, they therefore turned north again and at 21.15 circled RAF Chivenor, subsequently firing a red and white Very cartridge. The aircraft made a wheels-down landing but the aerodrome defence company had the impression that the crew had then realised their mistake and were about to take-off again, so a tommy-gun burst was fired at the cockpit, slightly wounding Obergefreiter Kurz. The aircraft was repaired on site and flown, with a Hudson escort, to No. 1426 (EAC) Flight, Duxford, via the RAE, on 11 December, 1941, in British markings and with serial HM509. On 1 July, 1942, it reverted to German markings, probably coded M2-M, flying sequences in the film *In Which We Serve* then in production at RAF Fowlmere, reverting again to British markings on 5 July. It remained with No. 1426 Flight until 26 July, 1944, when it was struck off charge.

Junkers Ju 88A-5 HM509 being inspected by USAAF personnel at Collyweston. It is in the revised paint scheme of dark green and dark earth top surfaces, with yellow undersurfaces.

Junkers Ju 88A-6, c/n 2492, at the RAE in about 1945. (*RAE*)

Ju 88A-5 (c/n 6214)

V4-GS of 8/KG1. Landed at RAF Steeple Morden at 04.30 on 16 February, 1941, with engine trouble after a bombing attack on Liverpool. Dismantled and removed to the RAE on 7 May, being reassembled, minus wings, on 14 June. Allotted serial HX360 and taken to No. 1426 (EAC) Flight at Duxford on 12 June, 1942, being used as a source of spares for the Ju 88A-5s HM509 (c/n 6073) and EE205 (c/n 3457).

Ju 88A-6 (c/n 2492)

Little is known about this aircraft except that it was allocated Air Ministry number 77 and exhibited at the RAE as the lower component of a Mistel composite aircraft. The upper component was the Focke-Wulf Fw 190A-8/R6 (c/n 733682).

Junkers Ju 88A-6/U Air Ministry 112 at the RAE in November 1945. Note the RAF roundels superimposed on the German Balkan cross, and the antennae of the FuG 200 Hohentwiel search radar. (*RAE*)

69

Ju 88A-6/U

This aircraft had been modified for long-range maritime work and fitted with FuG 200 Hohentwiel radar and two drop-tanks inboard of the engine nacelles. Allocated Air Ministry number 112 after capture, it was exhibited at the RAE in October/November 1945 and at RNAS Gosport on 11 September, 1946. It carried the letters MN aft of the fuselage roundel.

Ju 88A-12

1H-FF of V Gruppe Stab/KG26, with individual number 9 on nose. This dual-control trainer was captured in 1945 and had RAF markings superimposed on those of the Luftwaffe.

Ju 88G-1 (c/n 712273)

4R-UR of 7/NJG2, based at Volkel in the Netherlands. This was one of the more important German aircraft which came into Allied hands, for it was equipped with the FuG 220 Lichtenstein SN-2 and FuG 227 Flensburg radars which German night fighter forces were using so successfully to intercept the aircraft of RAF Bomber Command.

This Ju 88 was being flown on a North Sea night fighter patrol by Unteroffizier Hans Maeckle in the early hours of 13 July, 1944, when for some reason he made the error of flying a reciprocal compass course and landed the aircraft intact at Woodbridge emergency landing ground in Suffolk. With an escort of two Spitfires, the aircraft was flown from Woodbridge to the RAE via Hatfield by Wing Cmdr 'Roly' Falk on 15 July

Junkers Ju 88G-1, c/n 712273, TP190, with RAF markings and the yellow prototype letter P superimposed on blue-grey mottled upper surfaces and blue undersurfaces.

and allocated serial TP190 and, later, Air Ministry number 231.

Study of this aircraft's radars made it possible, within ten days of its capture, for Bomber Command to jam the Luftwaffe's SN-2 equipment, while the removal of Monica tail warning radar from British bombers rendered the German Flensburg equipment useless.

Soon after its capture this Ju 88 was repainted with German markings and the code 3K-MH and used in the making of an AI Mk.10 radar training film. It was transferred to the Enemy Aircraft Flight, Central Fighter Establishment, Tangmere, on 17 May, 1945, and the author saw the aircraft at North Weald in June 1945. This Ju 88 was tested at the RAE by Flt Lt D. G. M. Gough on 11 October, and it was on exhibition at Farnborough in that and the following month before being transferred to No. 47 MU Sealand for storage.

Ju 88G-6 (c/n 621965)

This aircraft, allocated Air Ministry number 9 and serial VL991, was at the RAE on 27 July, 1945. It was later flown to No. 6 MU Brize Norton and returned to the RAE on 30 August for instrument flying. The aircraft was scrapped in March 1950.

·Ju 88G-6 (c/n 623193)

This Ju 88 was flown from Karup (Grove) to Schleswig on 22 June, 1945, and on the following day from Schleswig to Gilze-Rijen in the Netherlands. It had been flight-tested by Flt Lt D. G. M. Gough on 13 June and allocated Air Ministry number 31. This Ju 88G-6 was one of the exhibits in the German Aircraft Exhibition at Farnborough in October/November 1945.

Ju 88G-6

This example, allotted Air Ministry number 1, was tested by Flt Lt D. G. M. Gough on 16 June, 1945, and held by the Enemy Aircraft Flight, Central Fighter Establishment, Tangmere.

Ju 88G-6

Allotted Air Ministry number 15. Nothing is known about this aircraft except that it was flown from Eggebeck to Schleswig on 14 June, 1945.

Ju 88G-6

Allotted Air Ministry number 16. All that is known of this aircraft is that it was flown from Eggebeck to Schleswig by Flt Lt D. G. M. Gough on 15 June, 1945, and from Schleswig to Tangmere on the following day.

Ju 88G-6

Allotted Air Ministry number 32. Two air tests of this aircraft were made by Flt Lt D. G. M. Gough at Karup (Grove) on 12 June, 1945, and the next day it was flown to Schleswig. After a further test on 25 September it was ferried to RAF West Raynham. The aircraft crashed on 15 October, 1945.

Ju 88G-6

This aircraft, with the code letters CB, was flown from Schleswig to Gilze-Rijen on 4 June, 1945, and from there to Tangmere on 7 June.

Ju 88G (c/n 620788)

All that is known about this example is that it carried the German radio code NF-DW and was allotted Air Ministry number 14.

Ju 88G (c/n 622138)

4R-BA of Geschwader Stab/NJG2, with VDR on the fin in white. This aircraft, which was at the A & AEE Boscombe Down, 1945–47, is believed to have been a G-7 sub-type with the radar aerial array removed.

Junkers Ju 88G, c/n 622138, at the A & AEE on 10 November, 1946. It has two-tone blue mottled camouflage on the top surfaces and blue undersurfaces with BA in black, and RAF markings superimposed on those of the Luftwaffe.

Ju 88G

This unidentified aircraft was allotted Air Ministry number 33 and operated by the Fighter Interception Development Unit.

Ju 88G-7a (c/n 621642)

D5-GH of 1/NJG3. This night fighter, equipped with FuG 220 Lichtenstein SN-2 radar, was landed intact at the Irish Air Corps base at Gormanstown, near Dublin, in the early hours of a May morning in 1945.

Junkers Ju 88G-7a, c/n 621642, VK888 at Tangmere.

On 2 June it was flown via RAF Valley to the RAE by Lt-Cmdr E. M. Brown. It was allotted serial number VK888 and was still on charge at the Enemy Aircraft Flight, Central Fighter Establishment, Tangmere, on 7 August, 1947.

Ju 88G-7b

This example had been operated by NJG4, the first half of its code being 3C, and it was fitted with FuG 218 Neptun radar with Morgenstern aerial array, elements of which were partially enclosed in a wooden nose cone. It was at RNAS Ford and Gosport, 1945–46.

Ju 88G-7c (c/n 622838)

An ex-NJG4 aircraft, this was exhibited in its original German markings at the Battle of Britain display in Hyde Park, London, in September 1945. It

Junkers Ju 88G-7b at RNAS Ford in the summer of 1945. It has two-tone mottled blue-grey top surfaces and blue undersurfaces with RAF markings superimposed. Part of its old code, 3C, can be seen aft of the fuselage roundel. (*Newark Air Museum 5950*)

Junkers Ju 88G-7c, c/n 622838, on display in Hyde Park in September 1945. It has two-tone blue-grey top surfaces, blue undersurfaces, and darker mottled fin.

Junkers Ju 88G-7c, c/n 622838, Air Ministry 48 at the RAE in November 1945. FuG 240 Berlin N-1a radar is installed in the nose cone. The small G on the nose is an original Luftwaffe marking. (*RAE*)

was allotted Air Ministry number 48 and had the letters MN aft of the fuselage roundel when exhibited at the Enemy Aircraft Exhibition at the RAE, Farnborough in October/November 1945.

Ju 88R-1 (c/n 360043)

D5-EV of 10/NJG3. This was another important 'capture' for the Royal Air Force. This particular Ju 88 was equipped with the then new FuG 202 Lichtenstein BC radar and, presumably by prior arrangement, was flown from Kristiansand (Kjevik) in Norway to RAF Dyce, now Aberdeen Airport, landing there at 16.00 on 9 May, 1943. It was 'intercepted' and escorted to Dyce by three Spitfires after crossing the coast about 15 miles north of Aberdeen.

The Ju 88 was flown to the RAE by Sq Ldr Kalpass on 14 May and used extensively by W and E (Wireless and Electrical) Flight on radar and radio investigation work, operating from Farnborough and Hartford Bridge

Junkers Ju 88R-1, c/n 360043, D5-EV at RAF Dyce, Aberdeen, in May 1943. (*IWM CH15679*)

Junkers Ju 88R-1, c/n 360043, at the RAE, with the antennae of the FuG 202 removed. Upper surfaces were black-green and undersurfaces light blue. RAF roundels have been superimposed, and the small code D5 is still carried ahead of the fuselage roundel. The Englandblitz insignia, carried by the majority of Nachtjagdgeschwader, was, at this stage, retained. (*RAE*)

Junkers Ju 88R-1, c/n 360043 as PJ876, at Biggin Hill in May 1961.

The Junkers Ju 88R-1, restored as D5-EV, at St Athan.

(now Blackbushe). The aircraft was given the serial PJ876 and first flown with this identity on 26 May. Flown by Sq Ldr Hartley, with Wing Cmdr Jackson operating the radar, this Ju 88 was used for extensive trials with Bomber Development Unit. These trials included mock combat with a Halifax but were brought to an end in July because of a blown cylinder head on one of the Ju 88's engines. The aircraft was flying again by 8 September on which date it was used for flame damping tests by the A & AEE at Hartford Bridge.

The Ju 88 was delivered to No. 1426 (EAC) Flight, Collyweston, on 6 May, 1944, at which time it was camouflaged with dark green and dark earth on the upper surfaces, had yellow undersurfaces and a yellow prototype P ahead of the fuselage roundel. On 31 January, 1945, the aircraft was transferred to the Enemy Aircraft Flight, Central Fighter Establishment, Tangmere, and given the identification EA-11. It was put into store at No. 47 MU Sealand on 1 November, 1945, and was at Fulbeck in about 1949 after which it was exhibited at a number of places including Biggin Hill. The aircraft was still at St Athan in 1976.

Ju 88R-2

3K-MH of Minensuchsgruppe. This aircraft was operated by the Air Fighting Development Unit at RAF Wittering in about 1944. The R-2 suffix has not been confirmed.

Ju 88S-1

This high-altitude bomber version of the Ju 88 was captured intact at Villacoublay, near Paris, in September 1944 and air tested there on 22 September by Flt Lt E. R. Lewendon. Allotted serial TS472, it was flown from Villacoublay to Hawkinge by Flt Lt E. R. Lewendon, with an escort of two Spitfires, on 24 September, and on the following day delivered to No. 1426 (EAC) Flight, Collyweston. Flt Lt D. G. M. Gough took the

Junkers Ju 88S-1 TS472 at Collyweston.

Ju 88S-1 on an air and electrical test on 2 November, and it was used for some local flying on 22 January, 1945. It was officially transferred to the Enemy Aircraft Flight, Central Fighter Establishment, Tangmere, on 31 January but not actually flown there until 18 April. It went to No. 47 MU Sealand for storage on 1 November, 1945.

This Ju 88 had blue-grey mottled upper surfaces and blue undersurfaces and, when captured, had the code 8E-MT or 8F-MT on the fuselage. Although KG1 and KG66 operated Ju 88S-1s, no Luftwaffe unit is known to have used these code letters.

Ju 88

A Ju 88, allotted Air Ministry number 2, was held by the Radio Warfare Establishment but nothing is known about this aircraft.

In addition to the Ju 88s detailed, it is known that two Ju 88Gs were allotted Air Ministry numbers 3 and 41. One of these, equipped with FuG 220 Lichtenstein SN-2 radar, was the Ju 88G-7a 7J-GH of NJG102 and it bore a small letter G on its nose.

Air Ministry number 47 and the serials VM865, VM870, VM874 and VN874 were allotted to unidentified Ju 88s. It is also known that Ju 88 c/n 622811 was flown from the RAE to No. 6 MU Brize Norton on 30 August, 1945, and that c/n 0660 was flown from the RAE to RNAS Gosport on 18 December, 1945, but nothing else is known about these aircraft.

Ju 188

The Ju 188 was a logical development of the basic Ju 88 and was produced in bomber and reconnaissance versions. At least six examples were examined or evaluated in the United Kingdom, and in addition to those detailed below, serial VH610 and Air Ministry number 45 were allotted, but to which specific Ju 188 airframes is not known.

Ju 188 (c/n 150245)

This aircraft was captured in about 1945 and is believed to have been allocated Air Ministry number 35. It was subsequently sent to the United States and the fin and tail cone are in the possession of the Smithsonian Institution.

Ju 188 (c/n 190335)

This aircraft was operated by 9/KG26. It took-off from Trondheim (Vaernes), ostensibly bound for Bardufoss in northern Norway, but flying at 50 ft it made landfall at Inverallochy, a few miles east of Fraserburgh where it landed intact on 2 May, 1945. It was flown to the RAE and was at No. 6 MU Brize Norton between the end of May and 22 July.

Ju 188A-2 (c/n 0327)

1H-GT of 9/KG26. This aircraft was allotted Air Ministry number 113 and serial VN143 and was at the RAE in about 1945. Between 11 September, 1946, and 11 August, 1947, it was at RNAS Gosport.

Junkers Ju 188A-2 Air Ministry 113 at the RAE. (*RAE*)

Ju 188A-2 (c/n 230776)

This aircraft was allotted Air Ministry number 108 and exhibited at the RAE in October/November 1945, with dark green upper surfaces and light green undersurfaces. The spinners were dark green with white spiral markings.

Ju 188D-1 or D-2 (c/n 0579)

8H-OH of 1/Aufkl Gr 33. This aircraft was captured towards the end of the war but nothing else is known about it.

Junkers Ju 188D-1/D-2, c/n 0579. It has grey and pale blue disruptive waveform camouflage. The O is white and the H black.

Ju 188E-1 (c/n 280032)

This example was captured at Fassberg in 1945 and used late that year for testing captured German bombs. The aircraft bore the code F2 forward of the roundel on the port side and UN aft of the roundel on the starboard side. It is possible that its full German identification was F2-UN but no Luftwaffe unit is known to have used this code. The aircraft was flown to the United Kingdom and was at the A & AEE at Boscombe Down, possibly until 1947.

Junkers Ju 188E-1, c/n 280032, at the A & AEE on 10 November, 1946. It has black-green and black top surfaces, and light blue undersurfaces.

Ju 290

Three examples of this four-engined maritime patrol bomber and transport are known to have been examined in the United Kingdom. Air Ministry number 6 was allotted to the first example acquired in 1945, but no other details are available.

Junkers Ju 290A-3 Air Ministry 57 at the RAE in November 1945. (*RAE*)

Ju 290A-3 (c/n 0161)

This Ju 290 originally carried the factory code SB-QK but became Red D of 1/FAGr 5 based at Mont de Marsan, south of Bordeaux. After capture it was allotted Air Ministry number 57 and exhibited at the RAE in October/ November 1945 with dark green upper surfaces and light green undersurfaces. The letters BK appeared ahead of the fuselage roundel.

Ju 290A-7 (c/n 0186)

This aircraft bore the factory code KR-LQ, and was flown from the RAE to No. 6 MU Brize Norton on 17 August, 1945. No other details are known.

Ju 352 Herkules

Designed as a potential successor to the obsolescent Ju 52/3m, making use of low priority materials, but only 43 production aircraft were completed. Three of the five captured examples, Air Ministry 18, 19 and 110, were employed on transport duties, including the ferrying home to the United Kingdom of released prisoners of war in June 1945.

Junkers Ju 352A-1, believed to be Air Ministry 18, at Knokke, Belgium, in about 1945. (*Newark Air Museum 7267*)

Ju 352A-1

This was the first example of the type captured, and it was used on transport flights by the General Duties Flight, RAE, between July and November 1945, with Air Ministry number 8. Before capture this aircraft had been operated by Transport-Geschwader 4.

Ju 352A-1

Allotted Air Ministry number 109 and serial VP550, this aircraft was exhibited at the RAE in October/November 1945, camouflaged with black-green top surfaces, light blue undersurfaces and yellow lower wing engine cowlings. The swastika was retained on the fin but RAF roundels were superimposed on the Balkan Cross, and in addition, the code RX appeared ahead of the fuselage roundel. Before its capture this aircraft was operated by Transport-Geschwader 4.

Junkers Ju 388K-0 Air Ministry 83 at the RAE, Farnborough. (*RAE*)

Ju 388K-0

A progressive development of the Ju 188, the Ju 388K-0 was a high-altitude bomber, ten pre-production examples being built at Dessau. One of these was captured in 1945 carrying the factory/radio code PE-IF in black on the fuselage, with a white 6 on the rudder. Allotted Air Ministry 83, it was attached to the General Duties Flight at the RAE during the period September–November 1945, and was on display at the College of Technology, Cranfield, in 1948. As late as 1967 the College retained the starboard nacelle and undercarriage, plus the tailwheel assembly. It had black-green and dark green top surfaces, with light blue undersurfaces, RAF roundels being superimposed on the Luftwaffe Balkan cross.

Messerschmitt Bf 108B Air Ministry 84 at the RAE in November 1945. (*RAE*)

Messerschmitt

Bf 108B Taifun (Typhoon)

This four-seat cabin monoplane was designed in 1933, and before the war it enjoyed considerable success as a sporting aircraft. During the war it proved an ideal vehicle for communications and light transport duties, and after their capture at least 20 examples were pressed into service. Minimal information is available on the aircraft allotted serials VM495, VM502, VM508, VM851–862, and Air Ministry numbers 76, 87, and 89; but an aircraft carrying its original Luftwaffe code GJ-AU was flown from the RAE to No. 6 MU Brize Norton on 14 August, 1945; Air Ministry number 84 was exhibited at the RAE in October/November 1945, and it had dark green upper surfaces and light blue undersurfaces. The type name Messerschmitt Taifun appeared on the fuselage beneath the cockpit canopy.

Another example, believed to have been requisitioned by a Beaufighter pilot in Germany, and photographed at Northolt after the war, carried the serial R2101 although this originally belonged to a Beaufighter Mk.1F.

Three aircraft were in the United Kingdom before the war and were not ex-Luftwaffe aircraft, but details of their history are included for the sake of completeness.

Bf 108B-1 (c/n 1660)

Built at Augsburg in 1938 and registered D-IDBT, this aircraft was imported into the United Kingdom before the war and registered G-AFZO. It was impressed for military use on 23 September, 1941, and allotted serial ES955 although this was incorrectly applied as ES995. The impressed aircraft was initially used by No. 24 Squadron and then on 9 August, 1942, was transferred to the Station Flight, RAF Andover. It was with the Station Flight, Northolt, from 10 January to 22 April, 1943, and then was returned to Andover, at which time it was painted in high gloss blue overall. This Bf 108 remained in service until 24 May, 1946, when it was flown to No. 5 MU Kemble for disposal. It was restored to the civil register, as G-AFZO, on 19 September, 1946, but flown to Heston on 26 September still in RAF markings and its high gloss light blue. For some unknown reason it bore the registration G-AFRN until being sold to Switzerland in April 1950 as HB-ESL.

Messerschmitt Bf 108B-1, c/n 1660, G-AFZO.

Bf 108B-1 (c/n 2014)

F8-CA of Stab/KG40. Two members of the Luftwaffe decided to desert and stole this aircraft at Chateaudun, taking-off at 06.00 on 11 September, 1943, to fly to England. Flying at 3,000 ft, they headed for Selsey Bill, the nearest point on the English coast, and on crossing the coast fired red and white Very cartridges which they hoped would indicate that they had no hostile intentions. They continued their flight to RNAS Ford where they again fired a red and white signal when chased by a Mosquito and two or three Hawker Typhoons. The RAF aircraft opened fire and although they did not hit the German aircraft, its pilot appears to have panicked and landed without his undercarriage locked in the down position. In the crash landing the fuselage of the Bf 108 was badly damaged and the pilot was so severely injured that he died a few hours later. The other occupant received only slight injuries.

Bf 108B-1 (c/n 2039)

Built at Augsburg in 1939, this Taifun was imported into the United Kingdom, registered G-AFRN and issued with a C of A on 26 June, 1939. It was impressed in May 1941, as DK280, for the use of No. 41 Group, Andover. The undercarriage collapsed during a landing at Weston Zoyland on 8 September, 1942, and the aircraft was struck off charge, but by 30 November, 1943, it had been repaired and put into service with the

Maintenance Command Communications Squadron at Andover. However, on 20 July, 1944, this Bf 108 suffered an engine failure and crashed at Boughy Fall Farm, Colton, near Rugeley in Staffordshire.

Bf 108B-1 (c/n 3701*)

Registered D-IJHW, this Taifun was based at Croydon Airport for the use of the German Embassy. On 3 September, 1939, it was immobilized by driving a six-inch nail into one of the tyres and removing the valve from the other. Two RAF officers subsequently collected the aircraft to fly it to an RAF airfield, still with its swastika and German registration, but engine trouble developed *en route* and they force-landed in a field near the coast. While the two officers were trying to locate the trouble, a zealous soldier 'captured' them and proudly marched them into custody. It was some days before the misunderstanding could be cleared up, but the aircraft was finally delivered by road to No. 10 MU on 6 December, 1939. Impressed and allotted serial AW167, it was delivered to No. 110 (AAC) Wing on 30 June, 1940, being transferred to the Station Flight, Abingdon, on 14 July, 1940. It was again transferred, this time to Andover, on 1 July, 1942, for the use of No. 41 Group, later being stripped of camouflage and painted silver with the code S6-K of the Maintenance Command Communications Squadron at the same base. It was flown to No. 5 MU Kemble, for disposal on 12 August, 1946, and subsequently flown to Heston on 26 September and temporarily cannibalized to service the wrongly serialled ES995. Later, it flew as G-AFZO, until sold to Switzerland in April 1950 as HB-ESM.

Bf 109

First flown in September 1935 the Bf 109 was, by any standard, one of the most remarkable military aircraft, and one of the few to achieve truly legendary status. It was built in larger numbers than any combat aircraft before or since, it was to achieve a record for length of production unlikely ever to be bettered by another fighter, and it outlived in service virtually all its principal opponents of the Second World War.

Bf 109E

Black 9 of 2/JG71. This Bf 109E was the first Luftwaffe fighter to be acquired for test and evaluation by the Royal Air Force. On 24 September, 1939, it landed at Rimling near Sarreguemines in the Moselle Département of France. It was inspected by the RAF at Nancy on 3 October but damaged while being flown by a French pilot three days later. However, it was repaired and made airworthy, painted with French markings and had French translations painted on some of the instruments. On 22 December,

---

*The c/n is unconfirmed.

escorted by a Lockheed Hudson from the A & AEE and flown by Wing Cmdr J. F. X. McKenna, the Bf 109 flew from Coulommiers to the A & AEE at Boscombe Down via Chateaudun and Tangmere.

In March 1940 the fuselage was seen being towed tail-first on its own wheels by an RAF vehicle on the Bishops Waltham–Alton road in Hampshire, presumably bound for the RAE at Farnborough. After this 109's arrival in the United Kingdom it had had its fuselage lime-washed giving it a dirty brownish-yellow finish. In service with 2/JG71 the identifying figure 9 was outlined in white. It is not known what happened to this Messerschmitt.

Bf 109E

Black 2 of 8/JG2. Flown by Oberleutnant Carl-Heinz Metz, this Bf 109E landed intact at RAF Detling, at 14.30 on 5 September, 1940, and was removed to the RAE for examination.

Bf 109E-3 (c/n 1190)

Built by Erla Maschinenwerk at Leipzig in 1939, this aircraft was operated by 4/JG26 based at Marquise-Est. It had dark grey upper surfaces, light blue fuselage sides and undersurfaces, and yellow spinner, engine cowling and rudder. The black and white JG26 badge was carried on each side of the fuselage beneath the forward part of the cockpit canopy and there was a yellow, red, black and white tiger's head badge on the port side below the rear of the cockpit canopy. The aircraft carried a white figure 4 with black outline and, at some time, beneath this figure was the double chevron insignia of a Gruppen-Kommandeur—believed to have been Hauptmann

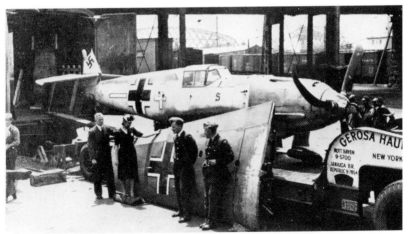

Messerschmitt Bf 109E-3, c/n 1190, arriving at the New Haven and Hartford Railroad freight yards at 132nd Street and Lincoln Avenue in the Bronx on 6 June, 1941, for exhibition in the USA.

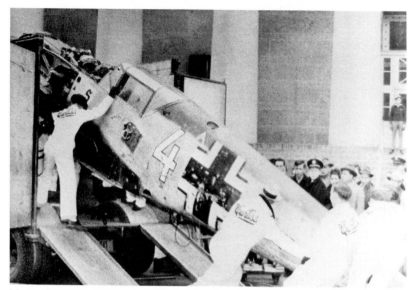

Messerschmitt Bf 109E-3, c/n 1190, arriving for exhibition at a site in New York. This photograph shows that the fuel octane triangle, above the white 4, contains the number 100, denoting that the aircraft was equipped with a DB 601N engine, using 95-octane C3 fuel, instead of a DB 601A, which used 87-octane B4 fuel. Although not confirmed, this would indicate that the sub-type was an E-6 tactical-reconnaissance fighter version, rather than an E-3. (*Thomas H. Hitchcock*)

Karl Ebbighausen of II/JG26. Five of his victory markings appeared on the fin (two Dutch dated 13 May, 1940, one French or Belgian dated 18 May, 1940, one RAF dated 24 May, 1940, and another RAF dated 14 June, 1940. The last is believed to have been a Fairey Battle or Boulton-Paul Defiant).

Unteroffizier Horst Perez flew this Bf 109 on a mission to England on 30 September, 1940. He was attacked by Hurricanes over Beachy Head and belly-landed the aircraft in a field at Eastdean in Sussex, causing only slight damage. The Messerschmitt was taken to the RAE and then sent to Canada and the United States where it was exhibited to help raise money for the Bundles for Britain campaign. It arrived in Nova Scotia early in 1941 and that June was exhibited in the New York area. At the end of the war it was delivered to the Arnprior Research Establishment in Ontario and in November 1966 returned to the United Kingdom. It was being restored at Hurn Airport, Bournemouth, in 1976.

Bf 109E-3 (c/n 1304)

White 1 of 1/JG76. Built by Gerhard Fieseler Werke GmbH. On 22 November, 1939, this aircraft was landed by mistake, because of fog, in an orchard at Woerth in Bas-Rhin in France. It was transferred to the CEV (French test centre) at Bricy near Orleans and painted in French colours

Messerschmitt Bf 109E-3, c/n 1304, in an orchard at Woerth, Bas-Rhin, on 22 November, 1939. It has black-green top surfaces and fuselage sides, light blue undersurfaces, the c/n and figure 1 in white, early type Balkan cross and black Swastika outlined in white.

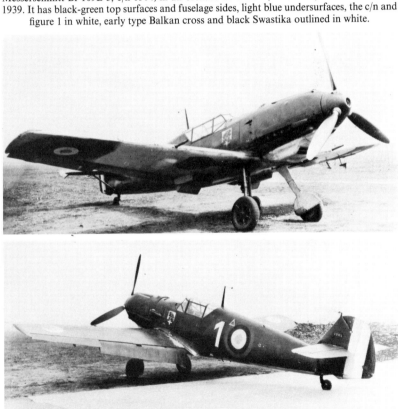

Messerschmitt Bf 109E-3, c/n 1304, shortly after its arrival at the A & AEE, Boscombe Down, still retaining its 20 mm MG FF cannon. Underwing finish should be compared with the RAE scheme for the same aircraft (*see* next page).

Messerschmitt Bf 109E-3, c/n 1304, at the RAE on 30 May, 1940, with all-yellow undersurfaces and no wing armament. The wing leading edges still carry the French inscription Ne pas pousser ici—Don't push here. (*RAE*)

The cockpit of Messerschmitt Bf 109E-3, c/n 1304, AE479. The photograph was taken at the RAE. Translations have been painted on some of the instruments.

Messerschmitt Bf 109E-3, c/n 1304 as AE479, at the AFDU, Duxford in about 1941 after fitment of late type Bf 109E canopy and new tail unit. It was camouflaged dark green and dark earth on the top surfaces, with yellow undersurfaces.

but retained its 1/JG76 insignia, constructor's number and white figure 1. In spite of several repaintings these German markings were retained.

The aircraft was handed over to the RAF at Amiens on 2 May, 1940, and that day was flown in mock combat against a Hurricane by Flying Officer M. H. Brown of No. 1 Squadron. On the following day Brown flew the Messerschmitt to the A & AEE, Boscombe Down, via Chartres and Tangmere, escorted by three Blenheims and the Hudson I N7205. The initial trials in the United Kingdom were undertaken by Flt Lts Tuck and Stainforth but most of the evaluation was done by Flying Officer Pebody.

On 14 May, 1940, this Bf 109 was flown to the RAE for general handling trials and in June was given the serial AE479. It was flown on cooling tests on 27 August and from 20 September until 20 November served with the Air Fighting Development Unit at Northolt. The aircraft was badly damaged at Farnborough on 5 January, 1941, when a tyre burst on landing, the tail being replaced with that from Bf 109 c/n 1480 formerly of JG3. AE479 went to the Air Fighting Development Unit at Duxford on 24 July, was transferred to No. 1426 (EAC) Flight on 11 December and, on 28 January, 1942, went to No. 47 MU Sealand for crating and shipment to the United States. It left the India Docks on board the ss *Drammesford* on 7 April consigned to Wright Field, Dayton, Ohio.

Bf 109E-3/B (c/n 4101)

This Bf 109 was built at Leipzig by Erla Maschinenwerk and when captured was Black 12 of 2/JG51 based at Wissant near Calais. It had previously served with 6/JG52. Before becoming Black 12 it had been Yellow 8 and earlier borne the radio code GH-DX. The yellow 8 had had a black outline and the black 12 a white outline.

On the afternoon of 27 November, 1940, this aircraft, flown by Leutnant Wolfgang Teumer, was over the Thames estuary when its pilot sighted three Spitfires. He released his SC 250 kg bomb, which fell into the water, before being attacked by one of the Spitfires. The Spitfire pilot scored a number of hits on the Messerschmitt and damaged its radiator, and Teumer was forced to make a wheels-up landing at Manston, with damage to the undercarriage and airscrew. The Spitfire pilot, a Canadian Flight Lieutenant, also landed to check that the German had been taken prisoner.

At the time of its forced landing the Bf 109 had black-grey upper surfaces which merged with the light blue undersurfaces to give a mottled appearance on the fuselage sides. The rudder was yellow.

Messerschmitt Bf 109E-3/B, c/n 4101, DG200 at the Rolls-Royce, Hucknall, establishment in about 1941. (*Rolls-Royce*)

The aircraft was taken to the RAE for examination and while there acquired from the extensive stock of ex-enemy Bf 109s a new fin and rudder from c/n 6313F (formerly with II (S)/LG2), a new upper forward engine cowling from c/n 1653 (formerly with JG51) and at least one new wing—it is thought that it had a port wing built by Gerhard Fieseler and a starboard wing built by BFW.

After being made airworthy this Bf 109 was allocated to the Director General, Research and Development, and on 14 December, 1940, delivered to Rolls-Royce at Hucknall. It was fitted with an oxygen system, was painted dark green and dark earth with yellow undersurfaces and given the serial

Messerschmitt Bf 109E-3/B DG200 at North Weald in July 1942. The cockpit canopy is missing.

DG200. It made its first flight with Rolls-Royce on 25 February, 1941, and was used on calibration tests before passing to the Controller of Research and Development and being based at Hatfield from 8 February, 1942. Some time earlier it had lost its original cockpit canopy, this presumably being removed to accommodate test pilot Harvey Heyworth who was over 6 ft tall.

The aircraft subsequently went to the A & AEE at Boscombe Down from where on 24 March, 1942, Flt Lt D. G. M. Gough was to have flown it to No. 1426 (EAC) Flight at Duxford, but because of a hydraulic failure it was delivered by road. After a major overhaul it was flown on a number of occasions before being crated for storage by the Imperial War Museum. Its engine was used as a replacement for one of those of the Bf 110C-5 AX772.

After the war this Bf 109 was put on display at a number of places including Biggin Hill, where it stayed for at least 10 years, with the code 12-GH. It has now been fully restored and in 1976 was at St Athan.

Messerschmitt Bf 109E-3/B, c/n 4101, after restoration at RAF St Athan.

Messerschmitt Bf 109E-4, c/n 3417, at RAF Detling on 30 September, 1940.

Bf 109E-4 (c/n 3417)

White 2 of 4/JG52. This aircraft, flown by Gefreiter Erich Mummert, made a wheels-down landing at RAF Detling on 30 September, 1940, after a combat in which the coolant system had been damaged. Streaming glycol, the aircraft nosed-over on landing and damaged the airscrew. This Bf 109E-4 had heavy dark green dapple camouflage on the fuselage and wing upper surfaces, light blue undersurfaces, and yellow engine cowling and rudder. The Staffel insignia, comprising a red cat on a white disc, was carried on the starboard side only. The aircraft was taken to the RAE for examination and was subsequently put on display.

Bf 109E-4/B (c/n 1106)

Yellow 1 of 3/JG53. This aircraft, flown by Oberleutnant Walter Rupp, was one of about 40 aircraft on free-lance patrol on 17 October, 1940. Flying at between 22,000 and 24,000 ft, the group was attacked by RAF fighters and split up, Yellow 1 and six others being separated. This Bf 109 was attacked off Gravesend by a Spitfire and the radiator was hit. The pilot tried to return to base but the engine overheated rapidly and he was forced to turn back, making a belly landing at Manston. The aircraft was taken to the RAE for examination and later put on display at a number of places including Tunbridge Wells. The aircraft's upper surfaces were dark green, the fuselage sides grey, the undersurfaces light blue, and the spinner, engine cowling and rudder yellow. A 250-mm red band encircled the engine cowling, the fin bore two white victory markings, and the yellow figure 1 had a black outline.

Messerschmitt Bf 109E-4/B, c/n 1106, arriving at Tunbridge Wells for exhibition.

Bf 109E-7/B (c/n 5567)

This aircraft of 6.II(S)/LG2 had black and dark green upper surfaces, mottled fuselage sides and fin, light blue undersurfaces and yellow rudder. Ahead of the Balkan cross was a black equilateral triangle with white outline and aft of the cross was a yellow C outlined in black. In the late afternoon of 6 September, 1940, this Bf 109, flown by Feldwebel Werner Gottschalk, left St Omer as part of a bomber escort. Flying at 12,000 ft near Chatham, the Messerschmitt was hit by anti-aircraft fire, the fuel tank being hit, and Gottschalk had to land at Hawkinge. Because of small-arms fire the pilot left the aircraft and ran to take shelter in a hangar, being wounded in the process. The aircraft was taken to the RAE for examination and subsequently put on display.

Messerschmitt Bf 109E-7/B, c/n 5567, at the RAE in about September 1940, with 6 Staffel badge, in black and white, carried on both sides of the engine cowling. (*Flight International 17993S*)

Bf 109E-7/Z (c/n 5983)

This Bf 109 was built by Wiener-Neustadter Flugzeugwerke GmbH and powered by a Daimler-Benz DB 601N-1 engine equipped with GM1 nitrous oxide power boosting. It was number 15 of 7/JG2, and on 9 June, 1941, flown by Oberleutnant Werner Machold, was hit by anti-aircraft fire and forced to land near Swanworth Quarries between Swanage and Worth Matravers in Dorset. The engine had seized, all the plugs on one side had been blown out and the radiator damaged by ground fire. When the aircraft landed it was found that the cockpit canopy had been jettisoned, that the windscreen was covered with oil and that all the guns had been fired. The aircraft, which had been attacking a Channel convoy, was taken to the RAE for examination.

Bf 109F-2 (c/n 12764)

This example belonged to I/JG26 based at St Omer and carried the double chevron Gruppen-Kommandeur's insignia ahead of the Balkan cross. It had mottled green/grey camouflage on the upper surfaces, light blue undersurfaces, and a yellow rudder on which 22 victories were recorded in red. On 10 July, 1941, flown by I/JG26's commander, Major Rolf Peter Pingel, the aircraft was pursuing a bomber over the south coast of England when it was attacked by Spitfires and forced to make a wheels-up landing at St Margarets Bay near Dover.

The Messerschmitt only received superficial damage in the forced landing. It was flown at the RAE on 19 September, 1941, as ES906 with the identification number 11, and on 11 October was delivered to the Air Fighting Development Unit at Duxford for comparative tests with the latest Marks of Spitfire. On 20 October the pilot was overcome by carbon monoxide and the aircraft crashed at Fowlmere in Cambridgeshire.

Messerschmitt Bf 109F-2, c/n 12764, at the RAE. (*IWM E(MOS) 335*)

Messerschmitt Bf 109F-4/B, c/n 7232, White 11, at Beachy Head on 20 May, 1942.

Bf 109F-4/B (c/n 7232)

White 11 of 10(Jabo)/JG26. This aircraft had a white bomb symbol aft of the Balkan cross and on 20 May, 1942, was flown by Unteroffizier Oswald Fischer as the leader of a pair engaged on attacking Channel shipping. While circling Newhaven harbour Fischer saw shipping to the southwest and made a low-level attack on a corvette. The bomb bounced over the corvette and as Fischer pulled up to clear the ship his aircraft was hit by machine-gun fire. The engine temperature rose to 160 deg C and Fischer had to make a wheels-up landing at Beachy Head. The aircraft was taken to the RAE and then delivered to No. 1426 (EAC) Flight on 21 August, 1943. One of the cylinder blocks was damaged in the Beachy Head landing, but a replacement engine was obtained from the Middle East and Flt Lt R. F. Forbes flew the aircraft at Collyweston on 24 October, still in Luftwaffe markings. Three days later it had been painted in RAF colours and given the serial NN644, but it retained its white 11 and bomb symbol. The Bf 109's port wing and aileron were damaged when it ground looped on landing at Thurleigh on 7 January, 1944. The Messerschmitt passed to the Enemy Aircraft Flight at Tangmere on 31 January, 1945, and went into store at No. 47 MU Sealand on 1 November that year.

Bf 109G-2/Trop (c/n 10639)

Yellow 6 of 3/JG77. This aircraft, built by Erla Maschinenwerk at Leipzig, was captured in Sicily in 1943. It was camouflaged with sand yellow and dark green mottling on the upper surfaces, had light blue undersurfaces, and black or black-green spinner, airscrew blades and wingtips. The yellow 6 had black edging, there was a white diagonal cross on a black disc aft of the Balkan cross, and the rear fuselage had the white encircling band denoting the aircraft's use in the Mediterranean area. The pilot's personal insignia was painted on the port side at the rear of the supercharger intake approximately midway between the windscreen and wing-root fillet—it comprised the Ace of Clubs, Ace of Spades and Ace of Hearts. The aircraft had under-fuselage pick-up points for a 300 litre drop-tank.

Messerschmitt Bf 109G-2/Trop, c/n 10639, being inspected before uncrating at Collyweston by Flt Lt E. R. Lewendon, *right,* and Flying Officer D. G. M. Gough. The Staffel insignia can be seen aft of the white fuselage band.

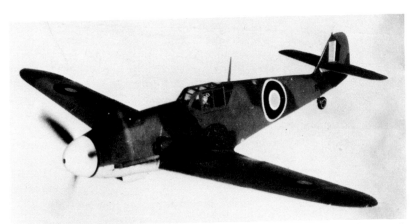

Messerschmitt Bf 109G-2/Trop RN228, with Flying Officer D. G. M. Gough at the controls in February 1944. (*IWM E(MOS) 1375*)

Messerschmitt Bf 109G-2/Trop, c/n 10639, finished as Yellow 14 of JG53.

Messerschmitt Bf 109G-2/Trop, c/n 10639, under restoration at RAF Lyneham in December 1974, before being moved to Northolt.

The aircraft was shipped to the United Kingdom, being received by No. 1426 (EAC) Flight at Collyweston, on 26 December, 1943. It was re-assembled and, still in its original markings, flown by Flt Lt E. R. Lewendon on 19 February, 1944. British markings and the serial RN228 were applied and photographic sessions for the Ministry of Aircraft Production were flown by Flying Officer D. G. M. Gough on 25 and 28 February. During 1944 this Bf 109 was flown on comparative and tactical trials against a Tempest V, a Corsair and a Seafire. It was transferred to the Enemy Aircraft Flight, CFE, Tangmere, on 31 January, 1945, and went to No. 47 MU Sealand for storage on 1 November that year. Later this Messerschmitt was displayed at various places with the codes C-25 and 8 and then as Yellow 14 of JG53. At some time a Wiener-Neustadter Flugzeugwerke manufactured tail unit was fitted. The aircraft was being restored to flying condition at Northolt in 1976.

Bf 109G-6 (c/n 163240)

Operated by 3/JG301 and having the manufacturer's radio code RQ-BK, this aircraft made a wheels-up landing at Manston in the early hours of 21 July, 1944, after its pilot, Feldwebel Manfred Gromill, had wrongly identified the aerodrome. Like the pilot of Bf 109G-6/U2 (c/n 412951), which also landed by mistake at Manston that night, Gromill made circuits of the aerodrome while flashing the aircraft's downward recognition lights.

Bf 109G-6/Trop

This unidentified aircraft was captured in the Middle East/Mediterranean area in about 1943 and may have been with I/JG77. It was shipped to the United Kingdom and arrived at No. 1426 (EAC) Flight, Collyweston, on 4 February, 1944. It was first flown on 9 April as VX101 but the use of this

Messerschmitt Bf 109G-6/Trop, later VX101, in its packing case at Collyweston in February 1944. (*Thomas H. Hitchcock*)

serial cannot be explained. The starboard undercarriage collapsed during a landing at Thorney Island on 19 May, and the aircraft was reduced to spares on 26 September. In the United Kingdom the aircraft had dark green and dark earth upper surfaces and yellow undersurfaces.

Bf 109G-6/U2 (c/n 412951)

White 16 of I/JG1.* This aircraft landed by mistake at Manston in the early hours of 21 July, 1944, after the pilot had orbited the aerodrome and flashed the aircraft's downward recognition lights. It was flown to the RAE by Wing Cmdr 'Roly' Falk on 26 July although two days earlier it had been allotted to No. 1426 (EAC) Flight. This Bf 109 was flown on a few occasions and then, as TP814, delivered to the Air Fighting Development Unit at Wittering on 31 August, where it was used for tactical and comparative trials against a Spitfire LF.IX, a Spitfire XIV and a Mustang III. On 23 November, 1944, the Bf 109 crashed while taking off from Wittering, but its pilot was uninjured.

Messerschmitt Bf 109G-6/U2, TP814, at RAF Wittering in about 1944.

When it landed at Manston this Bf 109 had dark green upper surfaces, light blue undersurfaces, mottled blue and green fuselage sides, fin and rudder, and bore the red Defence of the Reich fuselage band. It had previously carried the works radio code NS-FE.

Bf 109G-10/U2 (c/n 415601)

This aircraft was allotted serial VD258 and was with No. 1426 (EAC) Flight, Collyweston, in 1945. It was exhibited at the RAE in October/November 1945. In the United Kingdom it was painted in 2nd Tactical Air Force colours with black and white invasion stripes beneath the wings.

*This identification cannot be explained. All available information suggests that the unit was operating Focke-Wulf Fw 190s at July 1944.

Bf 109G-12

White 22 of 1/Jagdfliegerschule (fighter pilot school) 102 based at Zerbst near Dessau. The pilot of this aircraft decided to defect when a suitable opportunity occurred, and had memorized the bearing from Zerbst to Norfolk for this purpose. On the afternoon of 15 May, 1944, he was flying solo circuits in this tandem two-seat trainer version, and after his last landing he was ordered to make a flight of about one hour's duration, a drop-tank being fitted and the aircraft fully refuelled. The weather being favourable for his escape, a 10/10ths cloud layer between 2,000 and 2,600 metres, he left the Zerbst area at 17.10 and flew on a compass bearing of 284 degrees, keeping in cloud, but was able to identify Hanover and then the Zuider Zee through convenient gaps. He broke cloud near the English coast, lowered the undercarriage, and passed shipborne balloons near Lowestoft at 30 to 40 ft. He then climbed to 300 ft to cross the coast just north of Lowestoft. At this stage he had flown just over 700 kilometres and the warning light showed that his fuel was almost exhausted, he therefore retracted the undercarriage and made a wheels-up landing on a level piece of ground at Herringfleet Hill, near Lowestoft, at 18.57. Unfortunately, the aircraft overran the level ground and crashed into a ravine, the pilot sustaining a broken leg and other injuries. The aircraft was subsequently removed to the RAE for examination. At some time this Bf 109 had carried the works radio code DG-NR.

Bf 109G-14

This aircraft, a defection from 7/JG77, made landfall at 100 ft eight miles south of Aberdeen on 26 December, 1944, and flew to RAF Dyce but crashed on landing, turning over, and trapping the pilot who was subsequently freed and taken prisoner. Due to the arrival point and distance involved, it must be surmised that the aircraft came from Luftflotte 5 in Norway.

Bf 109G-14/U4 (c/n 541560)

This Bf 109 was found dismantled at Gilze-Rijen in the Netherlands, reassembled at Deurne, the Antwerp airport, by personnel of No. 1426 (Enemy Aircraft) Flight, and flown from there to RAF Hawkinge on 9 February, 1945, by Flt Lt 'Scotty' Gordon. On 24 March Flt Lt D. G. M. Gough flew it from Hawkinge to Tangmere where, on 26 April, it was taken on charge by the Enemy Aircraft Flight, Central Fighter Establishment, as VD358 and carrying the EAF identification EA-2. This Bf 109 was exhibited at the RAE in October/November 1945 and flown to No. 6 MU Brize Norton for storage on 10 January, 1946.

Messerschmitt Bf 109G-14/U4, VD358 (EA-2) at the RAE in November 1945. It has grey-green top surfaces, yellow undersurfaces, British applied 'invasion' markings under the wings, and Galland-type cockpit canopy. (*RAE*)

Bf 109G-14/U4

This Bf 109 was also found dismantled at Gilze-Rijen and after re-assembly, was flown from Deurne to Hawkinge on 9 February, 1945. On 14 February Flt Lt D. G. M. Gough flew it to Collyweston and entered the aircraft in his logbook as VD436, but its true identity was VD364. It was taken on charge by the Enemy Aircraft Flight, CFE, Tangmere, on 26 April, 1945, but while landing there on 17 May its port undercarriage collapsed after failing to lock down, and the aircraft was struck off charge.

Messerschmitt Bf 109G-14/U4, VD364, after its undercarriage collapsed and it had swung off the runway on 17 May, 1945. In the background is the wrecked Fw 190, c/n 180032 or 180082.

Bf 109K-2

Little is known about this Bf 109 except that it was captured at Fassberg, in Germany, in 1945 and believed to have been sent to the RAE, coded 44.

Bf 110

Another 'Maid of all work', the Bf 110 was in continuous service throughout the war, and production ran through six series from B to G for various roles including day and night fighter and fighter-bomber. Although in early encounters with Allied aircraft the Bf 110 did not show up too well, when used as a night fighter it proved more successful and its crews made a valiant attempt to stem the increasing Allied bomber offensive against Germany.

Messerschmitt Bf 110C-5 AX772 at RNAS Yeovilton.

Bf 110C-5 (c/n 2177)

5F-CM of 4(F)/14, built by Gothaer Waggonfabrik AG and based at Cherbourg. This aircraft was intercepted while on a reconnaissance mission on the morning of 21 July, 1940, and force landed in a beet field at Goodwood Home Farm near Goodwood racecourse. It had two-tone green splinter-pattern camouflage on the upper wing-surfaces, light blue undersurfaces, and light blue and grey mottled fuselage and tail unit. The letter C appeared in black beneath the wingtips.

This Bf 110 was taken to the RAE and repaired with parts from the Bf 110C-5 2N-EP which had been forced down near Wareham in Dorset on 11 July. The aircraft flew on 25 October, still in Luftwaffe markings, and performance and handling trials were undertaken at the RAE before it was flown to the Air Fighting Development Unit at Duxford as AX772 on 13 October, 1941. It was transferred to No. 1426 (EAC) Flight, then also at Duxford, on 5 March, 1942. At that time it had dark green and dark earth camouflage with yellow undersurfaces. This Bf 110 was transferred to the Enemy Aircraft Flight, CFE, Tangmere, on 31 January, 1945, where Commander M. A. Birrell DSC flew it in mock combat exercises against Seafire XV SR447 and a Mosquito FB.VI on 2 and 3 May. The aircraft was put into store at No. 47 MU Sealand that November.

Messerschmitt Bf 110C-5 AX772 with dark green and dark earth camouflaged upper surfaces, light blue undersurfaces and traces of the Luftwaffe code 5F-CM. (*IWM E(MOS) 1233*)

Bf 110C-5

2N-EP of 6/ZG76 based at Abbeville, but operated by III/ZG76 based at Laval. Flown by Oberleutnant Gerhard Kadow with Gefreiter Helmut Scholz as wireless operator/gunner, this aircraft was engaged in an attack on Portland in Dorset on 11 July, 1940, when it was attacked by a British fighter. After a short engagement both of the Messerschmitt's engines stopped and the pilot made a wheels-up landing at Povington Heath, four miles southwest of Wareham. After landing, the pilot was shot and slightly wounded while attempting to burn his papers. During interrogation the crew stated that the action was over so quickly that they did not open fire.

The aircraft was removed by No. 50 MU and taken to the RAE on 14 July. It was intended that it should be made airworthy for evaluation and the serial AX774 was allotted, but in fact parts of this aircraft were used to restore the Bf 110C-5 c/n 2177 which became AX772.

Messerschmitt Bf 110C-5 2N-EP at Povington Heath, Dorset, on 11 July, 1940. It has black-green top surfaces and fuselage sides, light blue undersurfaces, and a yellow E. There are two victory markings on the fin.

103

Messerschmitt Bf 110C-6, c/n 3341, on arrival at Los Angeles on 5 April, 1941. (*Lawrence J. Hickey*)

Bf 110C-6 (c/n 3341)

S9-CK of 2/Erpr Gr 210 based at Denain near Valenciennes. This aircraft was returning from an attack on Croydon during the evening of 15 August, 1940, when it was intercepted. The gunner was wounded and the undercarriage damaged and the pilot made a crash-landing at Hawkhurst in Kent, damaging the underside of the fuselage, the engines and airscrews. The aircraft was exhibited at Hendon on 24 August to help raise money for the local 'Fighter Fund' before being shipped to Los Angeles where it arrived on 5 April, 1941. It was reassembled and tested at Vultee Field.

Bf 110D (c/n 3339)

S9-CB of Stab I/Erpr Gr 210 based at Denain. This aircraft was also intercepted on 15 August, 1940, after attacking Croydon. Its gunner was killed and the pilot crash-landed it at Parsonage Farm, Hooe in Sussex. The letter C in the code was green.

This example was taken to the RAE and then shipped to the United States for testing by Northrop.

Messerschmitt Bf 110D, c/n 3339, at Hooe on 15 August, 1940.

The remains of Hess's Bf 110D, c/n 3869, at the Imperial War Museum store at Duxford.

Bf 110D (c/n 3869)

This aircraft had works radio code VJ-OQ and had been approved by the Messerschmitt works inspectorate but not delivered to an operational unit. Rudolf Hess, through his friendship with Willy Messerschmitt, made a number of practice flights in this aircraft and gave instructions that it should be fitted with extra fuel tanks. Using this aircraft, Hess set out from Augsburg at 17.45 on 10 May, 1941, on a misguided peace mission to Scotland. Hess jettisoned the extra fuel tanks on reaching the Scottish coast, and near Eaglesham, southwest of Glasgow, he baled out. The aircraft crashed at Bonyton Moor at 23.09 and was largely destroyed. The remains of the aircraft were crated and stored at No. 9 MU Cosford and No. 47 MU Sealand and the fuselage aft of the wing trailing edge was at the Imperial War Museum store at Duxford in 1976.

Bf 110D-0 (c/n 4270)

S9-DU of 2/Erpr Gr 210 based at Denain, near Valenciennes. Flown by Feldwebel Fritz Ebner with Gefreiter Werner Zwick as wireless operator/gunner, this Bf 110 made a bombing raid on aircraft factories in the Bristol area on 27 September, 1940. On its return from the target the Messerschmitt was attacked by Spitfires and crash-landed at Preston Hill, Iwerne Minster, near Blandford in Dorset. The observer was severely wounded. The aircraft was taken to the RAE for examination. The black letter D in its code was outlined in white.

Bf 110G-4 (c/n 180841)

G9-GR of 7/NJG1. Finished with two-tone mottled blue-grey overall, this aircraft was captured in Germany and is known to have been at Neumünster on 6 June, 1945. It is believed to have been flown to the RAE for examination.

Messerschmitt Bf 110G-4, c/n 180850, 3C-BA. (*Newark Air Museum*)

Bf 110G-4 (c/n 180850)

3C-BA of Geschwader Stab/NJG4. This aircraft, equipped with FuG 218 Neptun radar, was captured in about 1945 and flown to the RAE. It was at the Air Historical Branch's store at Fulbeck in 1949. This Bf 110 was given Air Ministry number 15 although that number had previously been used by a Junkers Ju 88G-6.

Bf 110G-4/R3

G9-AA of Geschwader Stab/NJG1, this aircraft was flown by Major Heinz-Wolfgang Schnaufer who later became Geschwaderkommodore of NJG4. This Bf 110 was exhibited at the Battle of Britain display in Hyde Park in September 1945 and is believed to have been allocated Air Ministry number 85. Inscribed with markings representing 121 victories, between 2 June, 1942, and 7 March, 1945, the port fin is on display at the Imperial War Museum in London.

The port fin from Major Schnaufer's Bf 110, detailing 121 victories, at the Imperial War Museum, London. (*IWM MH7232*)

Messerschmitt Bf 110G-4b/R7, c/n 730037, at the RAE in 1945. It was light grey overall with darker patches on the upper surfaces. (*IWM MH4904*)

Bf 110G-4b/R7 (c/n 730037)

This aircraft was captured in Denmark in 1945 and exhibited at the RAE in October and November that year. It was allocated Air Ministry number 30.

Bf 110G-4d/R3 (c/n 730301)

Believed to have been D5-RL of 3/NJG3. Equipped with FuG 220 Lichtenstein SN-2 radar, this aircraft was captured at Knokke in Belgium and flown by the RAE for evaluation in 1944–45. It is thought to have been allocated Air Ministry number 34 and was flown from the RAE to No. 6 MU Brize Norton for storage on 5 September, 1945. It was subsequently in store at Andover for more than 10 years and was still in existence at St Athan in 1976. For some unknown reason this aircraft appears to have acquired the code letters OL while at Andover.

Messerschmitt Bf 110G-4d/R3, c/n 730301, at Biggin Hill on 17 September, 1960, with two-tone mottled blue-grey top surfaces, light blue undersurfaces, and black code.

Me 163 Komet

Without doubt the most exotic aircraft to go into service with the Luftwaffe in the Second World War was the Me 163 ultra-short range single-seat home defence fighter which was powered by a single liquid fuel rocket motor, the duration being only about ten minutes on full power. But the Komet could climb to 30,000 ft in $2\frac{1}{2}$ minutes, and its maximum speed at that height was 596 mph. At the time of the German capitulation over 350 had been built and at least 25 were captured and air-lifted to the RAE from the British Occupation Zone during 1945, the majority from Husum, Schleswig-Holstein, being aircraft of II/JG400. The following Air Ministry numbers were allocated to Me 163s in 1945 but no details are available as to which specific airframes these were applicable: 200–202, 204–209, 211–214, 216, 218–222. Additionally, the following were at No. 6 MU Brize Norton on 22 July, 1945: c/ns 191095 (later shipped to Canada and now at Rockcliffe, Ontario), 191329, 191330, 191452, 191907 (later shipped to Australia and now in the National War Museum, Canberra), 191914 (later shipped to Canada), 191915 and 191916.

Me 163B-1a

This aircraft, with fuselage number 60, was at one time with 7/JG400. After its capture it was allotted Air Ministry number 210 and was at the RAE in 1945. It was later stored by the Air Historical Branch at Fulbeck and was exhibited at various places including Biggin Hill. The aircraft was presented to the German Federal Republic on 28 November, 1964, being completely overhauled at the Messerschmitt factory at Manching by a team of former Me 163 technicians under the supervision of Willi Radinger. Since 2 July, 1965, the aircraft has been on display in the aeronautical section of the Deutsches Museum in Munich.

Messerschmitt Me 163B-1a Air Ministry 210 in the Deutsches Museum, Munich.

Messerschmitt Me 163B-1a VF241, c/n 191060, at the RAE in about 1945. It had dark green wing upper surfaces and fin, the upper fuselage retained Luftwaffe two-tone mottled grey, and the undersurfaces were light blue. (*RAE*)

Me 163B-1a (c/n 191060)

This aircraft was flown from Germany to the RAE in an Arado Ar 232B-0 in 1945 and allotted an unrecorded Air Ministry number and the serial VF241. It also had a yellow prototype P aft of the roundel. This Me 163 was test flown from the Vickers aerodrome at Wisley in Surrey, being operated as a glider and towed aloft by Spitfire F.IXs which included EN498 and NH403. Lt-Cmdr E. M. Brown took the Me 163 on its first flight on 10 October, 1946, casting off from the Spitfire at 16,000 ft and remaining airborne for 25 minutes. It was subsequently flown from Wisley on 30 September and 3 and 9 October, 1947, before being towed the 120 miles from Wisley to Wittering on 1 November—the flight being made at 3,500 ft and taking 35 minutes. Two flights were made from Wittering on 13 November but the third, made on 15 November, ended in a crash-landing

Messerschmitt Me 163B-1a, c/n '191660', at the Imperial War Museum.

110

at 158 mph. During these unpowered test flights the greatest altitude was 25,000 ft and the highest speed was the 440 mph attained in a dive.

This Me 163 was for a number of years on display in the museum of the Royal Air Force College at Cranwell. It is then reported to have been presented to the Imperial War Museum on 27 July, 1962, but there is some doubt as to whether this was the aircraft shown at Lambeth. In the crash-landing at Wittering VF241 was badly damaged around the forward

Messerschmitt Me 163B-1a VF241. View of the cockpit with Mach meter at bottom left of centre panel. (*IWM MH12068 and 12069*)

fuselage and cockpit area but the example at the War Museum showed no signs of extensive rebuilding. Further confusion arises from the c/n 191400 on the port wing main spar and the c/n 191660 now shown on the fin. It may be that when No. 50 MU at Bicester was restoring an Me 163 for the War Museum it incorporated parts of VF241.

As exhibited at the War Museum the Me 163 was Yellow 3 of 1/JG400 and carried the Baron Münchhausen insignia of that unit. This aircraft was at the War Museum store, Duxford, in 1976.

Me 163B-1a (c/n 191316)

This aircraft was at the RAE in 1945 and in 1960–61 was refurbished by the members of the RAF Apprentice Training School at Halton and given to the Science Museum in London as Yellow 6.

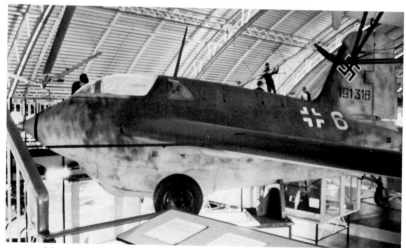

Messerschmitt Me 163B-1a, c/n 191316, at the Science Museum, London.

Me 163B-1a (c/n 191454)

Yellow 11 of II/JG400. This aircraft was at No. 6 MU Brize Norton in July 1945 and in September that year was exhibited at the Battle of Britain display in Hyde Park, London. It had black/dark green splinter-pattern camouflage on the upper surface of the wing and two-tone grey mottling on the upper fuselage, this fading into the light blue undersurfaces. The yellow 11 had grey edging.

Me 163B-1a (c/n 191614)

This aircraft was exhibited at the RAE in October/November 1945 and was still in existence at RAF Cosford in 1976.

Messerschmitt Me 163B-1a, c/n 191454, in Hyde Park in September 1945.

Messerschmitt Me 163B-1a, c/n 191659, Yellow 15.

Me 163B-1a (c/n 191659)

This aircraft was at the RAE in about 1945 and allocated Air Ministry number 215. It was presented to the College of Technology, Cranfield, on 14 May, 1947, and subsequently displayed at various places. It is now in store at East Fortune and bears the number 15 in yellow.

Me 163B-1a (c/n 191904)

This example of the Me 163 is known to have c/n 191904 although the port wing main spar carries the number 190596 and there is a metal plate in the cockpit bearing the number 316310/15. It was at the RAE in 1945 and allocated Air Ministry number 217. Later it was displayed at various

Messerschmitt Me 163B-1a, c/n 191904, Yellow 25.

places, at one time bearing the code number 82, and still exists at RAF Finningley, now with dark grey/green splinter-pattern camouflage on the upper surfaces and light blue undersurfaces. It bears the code number 25 in yellow.

Me 163B-1a (c/n 191912)

Exhibited at the RAE in October and November 1945. No other information available.

Me 163B-1a (c/n 310061?)

13 of II/JG400. This Me 163 was allocated Air Ministry number 203 and was at the RAE in 1945. It was transferred to the French Armée de l'Air and accepted at Dieppe on 10 March, 1946.

Me 262 Schwalbe (Swallow)

The world's first operational jet-propelled fighter, fighter-bomber and night-fighter, which would have been in service much earlier had it not been for vacillation and irresolution in the higher echelons of Germany and its aircraft industry. Nevertheless, over 1,400 were produced but only just over 200 were actually operational against the Allies. At least nine examples were captured in an airworthy condition and these were assembled at Schleswig and flown to the RAE over a ferry route, via Twente, Gilze-Rijen, Melsbroek and Manston, by a number of pilots, including the late Sq Ldr A. F. Martindale AFC, Flt Lt T. Melhuish and Flt Lt Pierre Arend.

Me 262A (c/n 500200)

This aircraft is believed to have been Air Ministry 79 and it is known to have been flown from RAF Manston to the RAE on 6 September, 1945.

Me 262A

This Me 262 was at No. 6 MU Brize Norton on 21 July, 1945, with the allocation Air Ministry 52, although this number was later allotted to the Bv 138B-1 VK895. The Messerschmitt was subsequently shipped to Canada.

Me 262A-1a (c/n 500443)

This aircraft was at No. 71 MU Slough in 1945, was transferred to No. 6 MU Brize Norton on 29 November that year, and passed to No. 47 MU Sealand on 1 May, 1946, for crating and shipment to South Africa. It was among the batch of German aircraft taken to Cape Town on the ss *Perthshire*. It was eventually given to a handiwork school at Benoni in Transvaal and used as scrap. By that time it was without wings but retained its original fuselage camouflage of dark grey mottling over very pale grey. The undersurfaces were grey and the tailplane dark green.

Me 262A-2a (c/n 111690)

Captured at Achmer in Germany, this aircraft is believed to have been operated by KG51 and was White 5. It was exhibited at the RAE in October/November 1945 with Air Ministry number 80—allotted later to an Arado Ar 234—and is thought to have been given the serial VH890. This Me 262 was at No. 6 MU Brize Norton in March 1946 and was subsequently shipped to Canada.

Messerschmitt Me 262A-2a, c/n 111690, Air Ministry 80, at the RAE in November, 1945. The fuselage is finished in dark grey, the wing and tail unit top surfaces are dark green, and the undersurfaces light grey. Air Ministry 80 and Figure 5 are white. (*RAE*)

Messerschmitt Me 262A-2a Air Ministry 51/VK893 about to become airborne from Farnborough, probably in 1945.

Me 262A-2a (c/n 112372)

Red X of 2/KG51. This aircraft was captured at Achmer in 1945 and operated by the RAE Aerodynamics Flight, being flown on handling trials by Sq Ldr A. F. Martindale in the period 11–16 October. It was allocated Air Ministry number 51 and the serial VK893. After disposal by the RAE the aircraft was placed in store, but later it was displayed at various places, at one time being painted to represent Yellow 7, an A-1a of III/JG7. With 2/KG51 the red X was outlined in white. This aircraft is still in existence at RAF Finningley.

Messerschmitt Me 262A-2a Air Ministry 51 on a test flight from the RAE in about 1945. The fuselage is dark grey, the wing and tail unit top surfaces dark green, and the undersurfaces light grey. Air Ministry 51 is white. (*Flight International 19003S*)

Messerschmitt Me 262A-2a, c/n 112372, (Air Ministry 51/VK893), masquerading as a Schwalbe of III/JG7, in a highly improbable colour scheme.

Me 262A-2a (c/n 500210)

Allotted Air Ministry number 81 and serial VH519 in about 1945, and subsequently sent to Australia. This aircraft is now in the National War Memorial at Canberra.

Me 262B-1a/U1 (c/n 110305)

Red 8 of 10/NJG11 based at Magdeburg. After capture this night fighter example of the Me 262 was flown from Schleswig to the RAE on 9 May, 1945. It was given Air Ministry number 50 and during the early summer was flown on radar and tactical trials at the CFE. On 6 July it was flown

Messerschmitt Me 262B-1a/U1, c/n 110305, at RNAS Ford in 1946. It has camouflaged dark green mottle on fuselage top and side surfaces, upper surfaces of the wings and tailplane in green, and black undersurfaces. The last three digits of the c/n, 305, on the nose cone are white.

(John Stroud)

117

Messerschmitt Me 262B-1a/U-1, c/n 110305, at RNAS Ford in 1946. (*John Stroud*)

from the RAE to RNAS Ford by Wing Cmdr Gonsalvez, passing to No. 71 MU Slough in 1946. It went to No. 47 MU Sealand on 8 November that year for crating and shipment to South Africa, arriving at Cape Town on the ss *Clan McRae* on 17 March, 1947. This aircraft is now in the Saxonwold Museum in Johannesburg and has been restored to its correct original camouflage and markings although at one time it bore the code EL-K. The red figure 8 is outlined in white.

Me 262B-1a/U1 (c/n 110635)

Red 10 of 10/NJG11 based at Magdeburg. This aircraft was at the RAE in about 1945 but nothing else is known about it.

Me 262B-1a/U1 (c/n 111980)

Red 12 of 10/NJG11 based at Magdeburg. This aircraft was flown from Schleswig to the RAE in 1945 and went to RNAS Ford before finally being destroyed at No. 6 MU Brize Norton in 1946 or 1947. The red 12 was outlined in white.

Messerschmitt Me 262B-1a/U1, c/n 111980, at RNAS Ford in about 1946.

Me 323 Gigant (Giant)

One of these large six-engined transports, probably of Transport-Geschwader 5, is reported to have landed at Christchurch, Hampshire, in about 1945, after flying from the RAE, although no relevant entry can be found in any Air Traffic Control log.

Me 410 Hornisse (Hornet)

At least six examples of this two-seat twin-engined fighter-bomber and reconnaissance aircraft were acquired for evaluation in the United Kingdom. Air Ministry numbers V2, 39 and 73 were allotted to three which have not been identified. In addition an Me 410A-1, c/n 10360, is known to have been flown from the RAE to No. 6 MU Brize Norton on 21 December, 1945.

Messerschmitt Me 410A-1/U2 Air Ministry 72, carrying c/n 420430 and code CC.

Me 410A-1/U2 (c/n 420430)

This aircraft, for which the c/ns 10430 and 10478 have also been reported, was captured in 1945 and is believed to have served in the Balkans. It is thought to have carried the works radio code PD-VO. It was allotted Air Ministry number 72/V1 and was at the Air Historical Branch's store at Fulbeck in about 1949. It was put on display at various places with the code letters AK and CC, and in 1976 was still in existence at St Athan.

Me 410A-3 (c/n 10259)

F6-OK of 2(F)/122. This aircraft landed intact and was captured at Monte Corvino in Italy. It is believed to have previously carried the works radio code SN-OK. The aircraft arrived at the RAE on 14 April, 1944, allotted the serial TF209 and flown by Wing Cmdr 'Roly' Falk on 1 May. It was

Messerschmitt Me 410A-3 TF209 camouflaged dark green and dark earth on the top surfaces, with yellow undersurfaces and yellow prototype letter P ahead of the roundel. (*RAE*)

damaged in a crash-landing at the A & AEE Boscombe Down on 5 June, but it was repaired and, on 14 August, flown to the Fighter Interception Unit at Wittering where it was used until 21 March, 1946, before being transferred to No. 6 MU Brize Norton.

Me 410B-6 (c/n 10278)

This aircraft was at some time with I/ZG1, based at Lorient. It came into British hands and was exhibited at the RAE in October/November 1945 with the markings Air Ministry 74/V3. This Me 410 was light grey overall with patches of medium/dark grey on the upper surfaces. The spinners were black with white spiral marking.

Messerschmitt Me 410B-6 Air Ministry V3, equipped with FuG 200 Hohentwiel radar, at the RAE in November 1945. (*RAE*)

120

Mistel S 3A Trainer Composite at the RAE in November 1945. (*RAE*)

Mistel S 3A Trainer Composite

Ju 88/Fw 190

This example of the Mistel composite aircraft was a 'mock-up' assembled by the RAE for the German Aircraft Exhibition at Farnborough in October/November 1945. It comprised Junkers Ju 88A-6 (c/n 2492) as the lower component on which was mounted the Focke-Wulf Fw 190A-8/R6 (c/n 733682). The Ju 88 bore Air Ministry number 77, was dark green on the upper surfaces and had light green undersurfaces on which was superimposed a black snaky pattern. The Fw 190 bore Air Ministry number 75 and was light grey overall with darker grey mottling on the upper surfaces. This Fw 190 is now in the Imperial War Museum at Lambeth.

Siebel

Fh 104 Hallore

One example of this five-seat twin-engined transport, of which 46 were built between 1939 and May 1942, was operated in the United Kingdom, in the communications role, in about 1945. It had Air Ministry number 119.

Si 204D-1

Operated by the Luftwaffe as a transport, liaison aircraft and trainer, the seven-seat twin-engined Siebel Si 204D-1 was acquired in some numbers by the RAF at the end of the war in Europe. They were used for

Siebel Si 204D-1 VN112.

communications and transport. Serials VM466, VM885–887, VN101–140, VN885 and VP320–339 and Air Ministry numbers 12, 13, 46, 49, and 55 were allocated, but in most cases it is not known to which specific aircraft these numbers applied.

Si 204D-1

BU-AP of Flugzeugführerschule (B) 5 based at Neubrandenburg. It was operated by the General Duties Flight at the RAE in July 1945, with the allocation Air Ministry 56.

Si 204D-1

BU-PP of Flugzeugführerschule (B) 5 based at Neubrandenburg. This aircraft was equipped with FuG 218 Neptun radar and served with NJG101 as a radar trainer. It was camouflaged with drab olive upper surfaces, had light grey undersurfaces, white spinners with black spiral pattern and black code letters. The aircraft was at Hendon on 15 September, 1945, and at the RAE that November, carrying Air Ministry number 4.

Siebel Si 204D-1 Air Ministry 56 at the RAE in about 1945. It is camouflaged drab olive on upper surfaces, with light grey undersurfaces. The code letter A is black with a red outline.
(*RAE*)

The following brief details are all that are known about other captured Si 204D-1s:

Air Ministry 5, operated by the RAE General Duties Flight and later at No. 6 MU Brize Norton; Air Ministry 28, c/n 221554, at the RAE in November 1945; Air Ministry 42, operated by Miles Aircraft Ltd and coded X; c/n 221558, was at the RAE on 17 August, 1945, flown to RAF Thorney Island two days later, flown to Rheims on 8 December, 1945, and returned via Eastchurch on 14 December; c/n 251462, was at the RAE on 23 October, 1945; c/n 251922, was at the RAE on 17 July, 1945; c/n 321308, flew from the RAE to RNAS Gosport and RAF Thorney Island on 31 July, 1945, and to RNAS Ford and back on 3 August; c/n 322127, flew from the RAE to Hendon on 14 September, 1945, returned to the RAE three days later, flew to Wisley on 26 September and returned the next day; c/n 324523, was at the RAE on 1 October, 1945; and c/n 351547, was at the RAE on 27 July, 1945.

This Fieseler Fi 156C operated by the RAF in the Middle East, retained the Luftwaffe code NM-ZS and had roundels superimposed on the Balkan cross.

Some Other Captives

In addition to the Luftwaffe types which were evaluated, operated and exhibited in the United Kingdom, RAF squadrons and personnel acquired examples in various overseas war theatres. These were mainly used in the communications role, but others were pressed into service as general hacks or used by the squadrons for evaluation against their own current equipment and then discarded. The variety and scope of these types was tremendous and only a representative cross-section is detailed here as the information is outside the scope of this book. Aircraft operated by the Commonwealth squadrons and the USAAF in overseas theatres are not included.

As an example of the variety of types operated, the RAF's Austrian Communications Flight, based at Klagenfurt after the liberation of Austria, had a Fieseler Fi 156C, a Junkers W 34, a Ju 52/3m, a Klemm Kl 35 and a Siebel Si 204A-1. The elderly W 34 had previously been operated by Versuchsstaffel 210 and still bore traces of its old code, 2H-OV or 2H-DV. The Siebel bore the number 168 on its nose and had been painted with black and white invasion stripes.

No. 111 Squadron captured a Focke-Wulf Fw 190 at El Aouina, the Tunis airport, in May 1943 and tested it against their Spitfire VCs. Another Fw 190 was acquired by No. 41 Squadron somewhere in Europe and this was painted in standard RAF camouflage and carried the squadron's code letters EB ahead of the roundels.

A Junkers Ju 52/3m was operated by the RAF from Foggia in southern Italy late in 1944. It retained its Luftwaffe code letters CQ-HH in black.

A Junkers Ju 87D-1/Trop captured and flown by No. 601 Squadron in the Middle East in about 1942–43. The squadron code UF is in white.

A Heinkel He 111P captured at Tripoli by No. 260 Squadron and operated as a communications aircraft in December 1941. At one time with II/KG4, it was finished in black and dark green splinter camouflage on the upper surfaces with light blue undersurfaces. The code letters HS appear ahead of the roundel.

This Junkers Ju 88D-1/Trop, c/n 430650, was in service in the Ukraine in 1943. A Rumanian pilot flew it by a round-about route to Cyprus and landed at Limassol in the summer of 1943. Given the serial HK959, it was flown to Heliopolis for evaluation after which it passed to the USAAF. The Ju 88 crossed the Atlantic via a southern route, arrived at Wright Field on 15 October, 1943, and was allocated Foreign Equipment Number FE-1598. It is still in existence at Wright-Patterson Air Force Base.

Messerschmitt Bf 109G-2/Trop, Black 13 of 2/JG27. Captured in Sicily and flown to the Safi strip, Malta, on 24 September, 1943, by Sq Ldr R. Webb of the RAAF, CO of No. 1435 (Spitfire) Squadron. It was originally camouflaged in sand with green mottle, had white fuselage band and wingtips, and subsequently acquired the name *Jack* ahead of the roundel and code letters AX of No. 1 Squadron, SAAF, aft.

In the Middle East and North Africa several examples of the Ju 87 were captured and flown. One was the Ju 87B-1, c/n 5763, which was being operated by the 209th Squadriglia of the Regia Aeronautica (Italian Air Force) when it ran out of fuel and force landed on 14 September, 1941. That October it was flown, as HK827, on fighter affiliation duties by No. 73 Squadron which was based at Heliopolis on the outskirts of Cairo. Another was the Ju 87B-2/Trop A5-HL of 3/St G1 which was captured in Libya at the end of 1941. This is now in the United States. A third was the Ju 87D-3/Trop S7-LL of 3/StG3 which was captured at Martuba in Libya in November 1942. This was test flown at LG 101 Sidi Haneish on 12 November, 1942, by No. 213 Squadron and the Ju 87 carried the squadron's code letters AK ahead of the roundels.

Another Libyan capture was a Messerschmitt Bf 110D-2 which had been operated by SKG 210. This was captured in about 1942 and reconditioned by the RAF—added to its nose was the name *The Belle of Berlin*.

Test and Handling Report Extracts

Messerschmitt Bf 109E-3 AE479

The Emil, as the E variant was nicknamed by the Luftwaffe, was flown by all three pilots of the RAE Aerodynamics Flight during May and June 1940, the total flying time during these tests being thirty-five hours. The aircraft was flown with tanks full at its full Service load, the all-up weight being 5,580 lb, which agreed well with the figure of 5,600 lb quoted by the Luftwaffe. The top level speed registered was 355 mph at 16,400 ft with radiators closed and 330 mph at 14,800 ft with radiators open, the absolute ceiling being 32,000 ft. A programme of handling and manoeuvrability tests was undertaken and the results of some of these are detailed:

Handling Tests:
    Take-off—All the take-off tests were done with the slotted flaps set at the recommended position of 20 deg. The throttle could be opened very quickly because the Daimler-Benz DB 601 engine was of the direct-injection type and responded almost instantaneously to throttle movement without choking. Initial acceleration was reported to be very good and there was no tendency to swing or bucket. During the ground run the aircraft rocked slightly from side to side but this was not sufficiently pronounced to worry the pilot. When opening the throttle the stick had to be held hard forward; the tail came up fairly quickly and the stick could then be eased back. The pilot was advised to hold the aircraft on the ground for a short while after he felt that flying speed had been gained because, if the aircraft were pulled off too soon, the port wing would not lift, and on applying opposite aileron the wing would come up and then fall again, with the ailerons snatching a little. If no attempt were made to pull the aircraft off quickly, the take-off was easy and straightforward, the run remarkably short and the initial rate of climb exceptionally good; in these respects the Bf 109 was classed as definitely superior to Spitfires and Hurricanes with two-pitch airscrews.
Time to Height:
    3,280 ft = 1 min 16 sec, 9,850 ft = 3 min 50 sec, 16,450 ft = 6 min 20 sec, 23,000 ft = 10 min 2 sec, 26,300 ft = 13 min 35 sec.
Approach:
    The normal approach speed was 90 mph with flaps and undercarriage down, the glide path being fairly steep and the view reasonably good due to the nose-down attitude of the aircraft.

Landing:

This was definitely more difficult than on the Hurricane or Spitfire, mainly because of the high ground attitude of the aircraft. The aircraft had to be rotated through a large angle before touch-down and that required a fair amount of skill on the part of the pilot; it also tempted him to make a wheel landing. If a wheel landing was made there was a strong tendency for the port wing to drop just before touch-down, and when the ailerons were used quickly to bring the wing up they snatched a little, causing the pilot to over-correct. By holding off a little high, the aircraft could be made to sink slowly to the ground on all three wheels, and there was then no tendency for a wing to drop. The pilots quickly became accustomed to the landing technique and had no difficulty after a few practice landings. The centre of gravity was unusually far behind the main wheels and in consequence the brakes could be applied fully immediately after touch-down without fear of lifting the tail. Due to the steep ground attitude and the consequent high position of the nose, the view ahead during the hold-off and ground run was extremely bad, although the run itself was very short and there was no tendency to swing or bucket.

Ground handling:

The aircraft could be taxied very fast without bouncing or bucketing but was difficult to turn quickly, an unusually large amount of throttle being necessary in conjunction with harsh use of the differential brakes when manoeuvring in a confined space. The brakes, foot operated, were powerful and could be used harshly without lifting the tail. Apart from turning, the ground handling qualities were good.

Stalling:

With flaps and undercarriage up, 75 mph ASI (indicated air speed); and with flaps and undercarriage down, 61 mph ASI.

High-speed dive:

AE479 was dived at 370 mph at which speed a considerable amount of pressure was needed on the left rudder bar to hold the aircraft straight. If the rudder were displaced in either direction and released, the aircraft eventually banked and turned to starboard. The rudder felt very heavy at this speed but there was no vibration, flutter or snaking.

Ailerons:

The pilots of the Aerodynamics Flight found that at low speeds the aileron control was very good; there was a positive feel and a definite resistance to stick movement, response being brisk. In these respects they reported that the Bf 109's ailerons were better than those on the Spitfire, which became so light at low speeds that they lost all feel. As the speed was increased the ailerons gradually became heavier, but response remained excellent. They were at their best between 150 mph and 200 mph and were described as 'an ideal control' over this speed range. Above 200 mph the ailerons started to become unpleasantly heavy, and at 300 mph were far too heavy for comfortable manoeuvring. Between 300 mph and 400 mph the ailerons were described as 'solid'; at 400 mph the pilot, exerting all his strength, could not apply more than about one-fifth aileron.

Fighting qualities:

Mock dog-fights were staged between the Bf 109 and a Spitfire both flown by pilots of the RAE. In addition, a number of fighter pilots, all of whom had recent operational flying experience, visited the RAE with their Spitfires and Hurricanes in order to obtain further combat practice. During these fights AE479 was flown by the RAE pilot, Flying Officer J. E. Pebody, who had completed the handling tests and was thoroughly familiar with it, and could thus be expected to get the best out of it. The arrangements were for the aircraft to take-off singly and meet at about 6,000 ft. The Bf 109 then went ahead and began to turn as tightly as possible to see if it could out-turn the British aircraft. After doing three or four tight turns in both directions the Bf 109 was put into a dive, followed by a steep climb. The aircraft then changed position and repeated the programme, after which the pilots engaged in a short general fight. When doing tight turns with the Bf 109 leading at speeds between 90 mph and 220 mph, the Spitfires and Hurricanes had little difficulty in keeping on its tail. During these turns the amount of normal g recorded on the Bf 109 was between $2\frac{1}{2}$ and 4g. The aircraft stalled if the turn were tightened to give more than 4g at speeds below about 200 mph. The slots opened at about $\frac{1}{2}$g before the stall, and while opening caused the ailerons to snatch; this upset the pilot's sighting immediately and caused him to lose ground. When the slots were fully open the aircraft could be turned quite steadily until very near the stall. If the stick were then pulled back a little more the aircraft suddenly shuddered, and either tended to come out of the turn or dropped its wing further, oscillating meanwhile in pitch and roll and rapidly losing height; the aircraft immediately unstalled if the stick were eased forward. Even in a very tight turn the stall was quite gentle, with no tendency for the aircraft to flick suddenly over on to its back and spin. The Spitfires and Hurricanes could follow the Bf 109E round during the stalled turns without themselves showing any signs of stalling.

After the turns the aircraft was put into a steep dive at full throttle with the airscrew pitch coarsened to keep the rpm down. It was found that both the Hurricane and Spitfire could keep up with the Bf 109 in the dive; the aircraft with constant-speed airscrews could do this more readily than those with two-pitch airscrews. The ailerons and elevator of the Bf 109 became so heavy in the dive that rapid manoeuvring was impossible. The Bf 109 was then pulled out of the dive and climbed at a very low airspeed at an unusually steep attitude. The aircraft was under perfect control during the climb and could be turned with equal facility in either direction. Under these conditions it outclimbed the British aircraft in most cases, since most of the British pilots climbed at a higher airspeed and a flatter angle, keeping below the Bf 109 and waiting for it to come out of the climb. However, pilots who chose to climb at very low airspeeds—mainly those with constant-speed airscrews—succeeded in keeping on the tail of the Bf 109, although its pilot thought that they would have difficulty in keeping their sights on him, as he was at a steeper attitude than their sights could 'line'.

In most cases this steep climb at low airspeed was the only manoeuvre whereby the Bf 109 pilot could keep away from the Hurricane or Spitfire. During the general fighting which followed the set programme, one other feature of advantage to the Bf 109 emerged. If negative g were put on the aircraft for a short time, the engine did not cut as it was of the direct-injection type; whereas on the Spitfire or Hurricane the engine immediately spluttered and stopped when negative g was applied, because the carburettor quickly ceased to deliver fuel under these conditions. Hence the Bf 109 pilot found that a useful manoeuvre when being chased was to push the stick forward suddenly and do a semi-bunt; if British fighters followed him their engines cut, giving the Bf 109 a chance to get away. This manoeuvre was particularly useful against the Hurricane, as its top level speed was less than that of the Bf 109, so that once the Bf 109 had escaped in this way it could avoid combat. The Spitfire, on the other hand, soon caught the Bf 109E after this manoeuvre.

When the Bf 109 was following the Hurricane or Spitfire, it was found that the British aircraft turned inside the German machine without difficulty when flown by determined pilots who were not afraid to pull their aircraft round hard in a tight turn. In a surprisingly large number of cases, however, the Bf 109 succeeded in keeping on the tail of the Spitfire or Hurricane during these turning tests, merely because their pilots would not tighten up the turn sufficiently from fear of stalling and spinning.

Dangerous manoeuvre:

During the general fighting, with the Bf 109 chasing a Spitfire or Hurricane, some of the pilots escaped by doing a flick half-roll and then quickly pulling up out of the subsequent dive. The RAE pilot flying the Bf 109 found this particularly difficult to counter, for when he rolled after his opponent, the speed built up quickly in the steep dive which followed the half-roll, and the elevator became so heavy that a quick pull-out was impossible; in addition, care had to be taken not to pull out quickly when the speed had decreased, because the aircraft stalled so readily under g. As a result, 2,000–3,000 ft might be lost in the manoeuvre, and if a Bf 109 pilot could be tempted to do this at low altitude a crash was almost inevitable. Conversation with some of the pilots who had had actual combat experience revealed that in several cases a Bf 109 had, in fact, been observed to crash in this way without a shot being fired.

General conclusions reached by the pilots were that they liked the positive feel of the ailerons and elevator at low speeds, and the excellent response characteristics of all three controls at medium speeds. The control characteristics which were particularly complained of, and which were considered to spoil the aircraft as a fighter, were: 1. Undue stiffening-up of the controls, particularly the ailerons, at high speeds; 2. aileron snatching caused by the slots opening during manoeuvres; and 3. absence of a rudder trimmer.

Aerobatics were another bone of contention; they were not easy on the Bf 109. Loops had to be started from about 280 mph, when the elevator was unduly heavy; there was a marked tendency for the slots to open near the top of the loop, resulting in aileron snatching and loss of direction, and in consequence accurate looping was almost impossible. At speeds below 250 mph when the ailerons were light and very effective, the aircraft could be rolled very quickly, but there was a strong tendency for the nose to fall in the final stages of the roll, and the stick had to be moved well back in order to keep the nose up. Upward rolls were difficult; the elevator was so heavy at high speed that only a gentle pull-out from the preliminary dive was possible, and a considerable loss of speed was thus inevitable before the upward rolls could be started.

Flying Officer J. E. Pebody, who flew the Bf 109 during these mock dog-fights, summed up his general impressions of the aircraft as a fighter in the following manner: 'From all this dog-fighting I am certain that if the pilot of a Hurricane or Spitfire finds himself attacked by a Bf 109 he can easily out-turn it, and can lose it straight away by doing any violent manoeuvre; the Bf 109 just cannot be made to do a really quick manoeuvre because at high speeds the controls are much too heavy, and at low speeds the slats come out, causing the ailerons to snatch, followed by the aircraft stalling if the manoeuvre is done more rapidly.'

During the dog-fights against the Hurricane and Spitfire it became apparent that these fighters could out-turn the Bf 109 with ease when flown by determined pilots. Since the minimum radius of turn without height loss depends largely on stalling speed, and hence on wing loading, the poor turning performance of the Bf 109 may be ascribed to its high wing loading, 32·2 lb/sq ft compared with 24·8 lb/sq ft on the Spitfire. The minimum radius of turn without height loss was obtained by flying as near the stall as possible at comparatively little g; this radius was about 696 ft on the Spitfire as against 885 ft on the Bf 109.

Assessment:

The tests brought to light that as a fighter the Bf 109 was generally inferior to the Hurricane or Spitfire. Its fighting qualities, good and bad, were detailed as follows:

Good points:

1. High top speed and excellent rate of climb; 2. good control at low speeds; 3. gentle stall, even under g; and 4. engine does not cut immediately under negative g.

Bad points:

1. Controls, particularly the ailerons, far too heavy at high speeds; 2. owing to high wing loading, the aircraft stalls readily under g and has a poor turning circle; 3. aileron snatching occurs as the slots open; 4. quick manoeuvres are difficult, because of 1 at high speed, and 2 and 3 at low speed; 5. absence of a rudder trimmer, curtailing ability to bank to port at high speeds; and 6. cockpit too cramped for comfort when fighting.

The gentle stall and good control under g were of some importance, as they enabled the pilot to get the most out of the aircraft in a circling dog-fight by flying very near the stall. As mentioned previously, Flying Officer Pebody, the Bf 109 test-pilot, succeeded in keeping on the tail of the Spitfire in many cases, despite the latter aircraft's superior performance in turning, because a number of the Spitfire pilots failed to tighten up the turn sufficiently. If the stick were pulled back too far on the Spitfire in a tight turn, the aircraft might stall rather violently, flick over on to its back, and spin. Knowledge of this undoubtedly deterred the pilot from tightening his turn when being chased, particularly if he was not very experienced. The most serious defect of the Bf 109 was its inability to roll fast in a high-speed dive because of its heavy ailerons.

Conclusions:

All three RAE test pilots gave their opinions on cockpit layout, comfort and convenience, and their views are summarised as follows:

Cockpit size: The cockpit was unquestionably too cramped for comfort. It was too narrow, the headroom insufficient, and the seating position tiring. When wearing a seat-type parachute a pilot of normal size found that his head touched the hood roof.

Noise: With the side windows open the noise in the cockpit was considerable. It was lessened by closing the side windows, but even then the cockpit was far noisier at full throttle than that of the Hurricane or Spitfire.

Main Flying Controls: The control column position was good and the slight offset of the grip was convenient. The position of the rudder pedals made for too reclining an attitude, putting extra weight on the small of the back; a bad feature was the absence of any fore-and-aft adjustment of the rudder pedals.

Trimming and Flap Controls: These were particularly well placed on the pilot's left. The flap gear was very good, for it was easy to operate and, being manual, was not likely to go wrong. The juxtaposition of the tailplane adjusting wheel and the flap control wheel was also considered an excellent feature, as the wheels could be operated together with one hand and the change of trim due to flaps thereby automatically corrected.

Throttle: The throttle arrangements were described by one of the test pilots as 'marvellously simple; there's just one lever with no gate or over-ride to worry about'. It may be mentioned here that, while the pilots were not greatly impressed with the Bf 109 as an aircraft, the Daimler-Benz DB 601 direct-injection engine came in for very favourable comment. The response to throttle opening was particularly good, it was apparently impossible to choke the engine, and there was no tendency to splutter and stop when the aircraft was subjected to negative g by suddenly pushing the stick forward.

Airscrew Control: This worked well, no difficulty being experienced during the tests. The pitch control lever would have been better placed alongside the throttle than on the dashboard.

Undercarriage Control: The undercarriage selector was free from complication and could not be criticized. The absence of an undercarriage warning hooter seemed strange to British pilots.

Brakes: These were foot-operated, they worked well; but the standard Dunlop system operated from a toggle on the stick was thought to provide a more sensitive control.

Instrument Panel: Except for the absence of a blind-flying panel, the instruments present were adequate and the grouping was good, flying instruments being on the left and engine instruments on the right. The absence of a gyro horizon was severely felt when flying in cloud but the instruments were clear to read. No flying was done at night, but the lighting arrangements appeared to be rather inadequate.

Ancillary Equipment: Guns, sights and radio were not tested. The radio layout appeared to be well placed, and the machine-gun and cannon firing switches, mounted in the grip of the stick, came readily to hand. The electrical panel on the lower right of the dashboard was considered difficult to use until the pilot became familiar with it, as the various press buttons could not be readily distinguished. An interesting feature was the jettison arrangements for the Very cartridges, designed to enable a pilot quickly to jettison the cartridges before a forced landing in enemy territory, so that he did not give away the signal of the day.

Cockpit View/Hood: The cockpit hood did not slide back, it was hinged at the starboard side for entry and exit, and could not therefore be opened in flight. Sliding windows were fitted, one in each side panel of the hood. The hood-jettisoning arrangements for emergency exit were found interesting, the hood was spring-loaded, and on pushing the jettison lever the whole of the hood and the radio mast behind it were flung clear backwards. The view forward when taxi-ing was very bad, partly due to the steep ground attitude of the aircraft, and partly because the hood could not be slid back to enable the pilot to look round the edge of the windscreen. When in flight, the view forward and sideways was normal, being similar to the Hurricane; the windscreen framework members were sufficiently narrow and did not catch the pilot's eye nor create blind spots. Sideways and rearwards the view was about the same as on the Spitfire and Hurricane, but the cramped position of the pilot in the Bf 109's cockpit made it difficult to look downward or upward to the rear, and the tailplane could only be seen with an effort. The direct-vision opening gave a large field of view and was completely draught-free at all speeds. A high speed could thus be maintained in bad weather conditions, whereas on the Hurricane or Spitfire the pilot had to slide back the hood and look round the edge of the windscreen to obtain a view forward in rain or cloud, and could only do this by flying at fairly low speed. The direct-vision opening also assisted landing, as the high position of the nose obstructed the view forward during the hold-off, and the opening was in the correct position to give a view of the ground. The windscreen panels were clear and free from distortion, and did not oil up in flight; it was found that the hood sliding panels were difficult to open, particularly at high speeds.

In addition to the official test report personal reminiscences of flying AE479 include the following:

Air Marshal Sir Ralph S. Sorley, KCB: 'I flew it at the A & AEE Boscombe Down where I was CO at the time, my logbook dates the flight as 12 May, 1940, and my comments were: Very nice and has points. Take-off quite normal but wants plenty of right rudder at unstick. Rudder light and quite effective. Ailerons good—light and effective below 300 mph but harden up above this speed. Very stable fore and aft—heavy on elevator and needs tail trim adjustment for each change of speed. Lands very normally and is nice on control right onto the ground. Seems to turn equally well to port or starboard but has a rudder of the old school and top rudder is needed on all turns. The worst features are poor forward view for sighting and landing, and a cramped cockpit. Engine is smooth and powerful and runs well, opens up instantly.'

Air Commodore P. E. Warcup, CBE, RAF (Rtd): 'I certainly flew it several times and I remember certain aspects of it very vividly. After its arrival at the A & AEE Boscombe Down, on 3 May, 1940, it was subject to a good deal of 'looking at'' and speculation was rife over one aspect in particular. The wing fillets had rubbed off a strip of paint on the wing!, no-one was quite sure why but it obviously indicated wing movement. I was astonished at the speed with which the Air Ministry produced the manufacturers handbook (within 48 hours), and the book proved that the wing was meant to move and thereafter no-one could see why it shouldn't be flown. I was in Sq Ldr Ramsbottom-Isherwood's Flight, which did the trials on fighter aircraft, and was detailed to fly it. It was a much smaller machine than the Spitfire, I had to take the sorbo-pad off my parachute and even then my head was hard up against the canopy. From memory we left the instruments alone and one had to interpret, providing the limits were known this was not too difficult. The engine had direct fuel injection and the throttle response was fantastic for those days. You could hit the throttle really hard and the engine responded, whereas the Merlin, given similar treatment, would have coughed and died. Flying controls and response were normal and unremarkable, except the longitudinal control was so heavy at speed it was difficult to loop the aircraft neatly. This defect was to save my life subsequently and undoubtedly must have saved many others. The airscrew control was worthy of note. The propeller acted like a fixed-pitch screw but you set the pitch for take-off, climb or cruise as required. Once set it remained in that pitch until you reset it. The pitch was presented by a clock face and you selected the "time" to suit the flight conditions. Remember the constant-speed propeller had only just been fitted to our own fighters. The aircraft had a 20 mm cannon between the cylinder banks firing through the airscrew, this was not fired during my time. The wings were fitted with automatic slots at the wingtips. It was docile at slow speeds and landing presented no particular problems except that my vision, for reasons given above, was not very good. Although the undercarriage was narrow the stability on the grass at Boscombe Down was good—not of course as solid as the Hurricane with its wide undercarriage. In short, an excellent aircraft except, in my view, for its longitudinal control. It was better in many respects than the Hurricane, and compared to the Spitfire it was probably livelier, and of course its throttle response gave it a great advantage, but I will never understand how the Germans accepted such longitudinal stiffness in a fighter'.

Group Captain S. Wroath, CBE, AFC, AFRAeS, RAF (Rtd): 'My logbook would seem to show that my first flight in it, at the A & AEE Boscombe Down, was on 8 May, 1940, in the afternoon, flight trial emphasis at the time was with its handling characteristics particularly in relation, naturally enough, to the Hurricane and Spitfire. Such people as Harry Broadhurst, Sailor Malan and others, came and flew it, and there was much discussion on it and its flight characteristics'.

Flying Officer M. H. Brown, No. 1 Squadron: (mock combat against a Hurricane 2 May, 1940): 'Although it appears that the spectators were more visibly shaken than the pilots, several valuable facts emerged. The Bf 109 had excellent rearward vision and proved to be unquestionably faster than the Hurricane at high altitude. To offset this, the Hawker machine was more manoeuvrable and slightly faster on the deck'.

Messerschmitt Bf 109G-2/Trop RN228

Comparative trials between this Bf 109G and a Tempest V, Corsair and Seafire were conducted during 1944. These trials indicated that the Tempest V, using 9 lb of boost, possessed a speed advantage of 40–50 mph at altitudes up to 20,000 ft, but that the speed advantage diminished rapidly above that altitude. The rate of climb of the Bf 109G-2 was superior to that of the Tempest at all altitudes, although this advantage was not pronounced at heights below 5,000 ft, but in comparative dives the Tempest proved capable of pulling away from the Messerschmitt. The turning circle of the Tempest was marginally superior and there was little to choose between the two aircraft in roll rate at speeds below 350 mph, but above this speed the Tempest could out-manoeuvre its opponent by making a quick change of bank and direction.

Messerschmitt Bf 109G-6/U2 TP814

Comparative trials flown at the AFDU, RAF Wittering, 1944.
Flying Characteristics:
The rudder was fairly heavy but not uncomfortably so, but as no rudder trimming device was provided it was necessary to apply right rudder for take-off and left rudder at high speeds. The ailerons became increasingly stiff as speed was increased and were especially so at speeds in excess of 350 mph. At speeds below 180 mph the ailerons were not positive and became non-effective as the stall was approached. The elevators also

became increasingly difficult to operate as speed increased, and above 350 mph this unpleasantness was accentuated as the elevator trim was practically impossible to operate.

The forward view for taxi-ing was very poor and was little improved in flight because of the gun magazine bulges on the engine cowling and the thickness of the windscreen framing. The brakes were positive but the tailwheel did not castor easily, and sharp turns on the ground were difficult. At all times when the engine was running at low speed the pilot suffered acute discomfort from fumes in the cockpit. Unless taking-off directly into wind, the aircraft had a strong tendency to swing into the wind, and the throttle had to be opened slowly. The tailwheel locking mechanism on this particular aircraft had been disconnected, and this increased the tendency to swing. When taking-off directly into wind the aircraft presented no control problems.

Comparisons with the Spitfire LF.IX:

The Bf 109G-6 was compared with a Spitfire LF.IX for speed and all-round manoeuvrability at altitudes up to 25,000 ft, and it was found that up to 16,000 ft the Spitfire possessed a slight speed advantage when using 18 lb boost. Between this altitude and 20,000 ft the Bf 109G-6 possessed a slight edge in speed, but above 20,000 ft the Spitfire regained the speed advantage to the extent of 7 mph. When 25 lb boost was employed by the Spitfire it was about 25 mph faster at altitudes below 15,000 ft, and some 7 mph faster above this height. The climb of the Spitfire was superior to that of the Messerschmitt at all altitudes, and the British fighter enjoyed a particularly marked advantage below 13,000 ft when using 18 lb boost, this naturally being even more pronounced when 25 lb of boost was employed. When both aircraft pulled up into a climb from a dive their performances were almost identical, but when climbing speed was attained the Spitfire slowly pulled away. Comparative dives showed that the Bf 109G-6 could leave the Spitfire without any difficulty, but the turning circle and roll rate of the Spitfire were markedly superior at all speeds.

Comparison with the Spitfire XIV:

The Bf 109G-6 was compared with a fully operational Spitfire XIV and, using 18 lb of boost, it was found that the Spitfire possessed an advantage in speed of 25 mph at altitudes up to 16,000 ft, this being the rated altitude of the Bf 109G-6, at which the advantage to the Spitfire was reduced to 10 mph. Above 16,000 ft the speed advantage of the Spitfire XIV increased progressively with altitude, being 50 mph faster at 30,000 ft. At the rated altitude of the Messerschmitt there was little to choose between the two fighters in climbing performance, but at all other altitudes the Spitfire possessed a marked advantage in rate of climb. When both aircraft were put into a dive with engine throttled back and then pulled into climbing attitude, their rate of climb was identical, but when using maximum power in the dive the Spitfire easily left the Bf 109G-6 behind in the subsequent climb. Comparative dives revealed that the Bf 109G-6 possessed a slight initial advantage but this was lost at speeds in excess of 380 mph. The

Spitfire XIV had no difficulty in out-turning the Bf 109G-6 in either direction, but the advantage was more marked when turning to starboard, this being due to the greater power of its Griffon engine at full throttle and to the use of a contra-rotating propeller.

Comparison with a Mustang III (P-51C):

The Mustang III possessed a clear speed advantage at all altitudes, this being some 30 mph greater at the Bf 109G-6's rated altitude and increasing to 50 mph at 30,000 ft. The Bf 109G-6 had a slightly better climb rate up to 20,000 ft, but between this altitude and 25,000 ft the Mustang had a very slight advantage. When the two aircraft were dived and subsequently climbed there was very little to choose between their performances. The comparison of the respective merits of the two aircraft in dives proved that the Messerschmitt was steadily out-dived by the Mustang, and the longer the dive the greater the gain of the latter. The Mustang had no difficulty in out-turning the Bf 109G-6 in either direction, and the rate of roll of the two fighters was almost identical.

Focke-Wulf Fw 190A-3 MP499

Comparative trials flown at the AFDU, RAF Duxford in 1942, with the Fw 190 flown by Flt Lt Clive, the Spitfire IX by Flying Officer Godefroy, and the Lockheed P-38F Lightning by Col Stone of the USAAF. A level run was made at a height of 2,000 ft for two minutes, after which the Fw 190 was leading and followed very close behind by the Spitfire, with the P-38 about 400 yards further behind.

The aircraft then re-formed in formation and carried out a climb from 2,000 ft at maximum continuous climbing conditions to 8,000 ft, time to this height being: Fw 190 = 1 min 45 sec; Spitfire IX = 1 min 45 sec; and P-38 Lightning = 2 min.

Indicated airspeed before commencement of the climb was 300–315 mph. The difference between the Fw 190 and the P-38 was about the same as at 2,000 ft, but the Spitfire IX was quickly drawing away and at the end of the run was 200 yards ahead. The aircraft then again re-formed in formation and made a dive together from 8,000 ft to 1,000 ft. The Fw 190 accelerated away at the beginning of the dive and remained ahead. The P-38 appeared to be catching up slightly at the end of the dive but its acceleration was not nearly as good. The Spitfire was left behind and although it appeared to be catching up slightly, it was likely to be out-dived by the Fw 190. The latter appeared to be running satisfactorily, although the engine was still rough when throttled back.

The Fw 190 and the Spitfire IX took-off to try jumping one another at various speeds at 2,000 ft and 8,000 ft. At 8,000 ft the Spitfire cruising at zero boost and 2,200 rpm, was jumped by the Fw 190, 2,000 ft above. When the Fw 190 came within 1,000 yards, the Spitfire was opened up to full power and put into a gentle dive, but the Fw 190 managed to catch it easily and the Spitfire was reduced to taking evasive action. This trial was to be repeated again and it appeared that the Spitfire must, while in an area where enemy fighters were likely to be encountered, fly at high speed. During this test the engine appeared to be rather rough, it was subsequently run up on the ground which proved there was no drop on the two magnetos.

Comparative climbs between the three aircraft started at 5,000 ft from approximately cruising speed, opening up to maximum climb to 18,000 ft, time to this height being: Spitfire IX = 3 min 17 sec at 9 lb boost and 2,650 rpm; Fw 190 = 3 min 25 sec at 1·3 lb boost and 2,400 rpm; P-38 Lightning = 3 min 39 sec at 37·8 inches boost and 2,600 rpm. The angle of climb of all three aircraft was the same, although the P-38 fell behind in the initial stages of the climb it was gaining as a higher altitude was reached. The aircraft then re-formed in formation at 15,000 ft and a straight run for two minutes gave the following results: the Spitfire was leading by 50 yards from the Fw 190, with the P-38 100 yards further behind. At 15,000 ft the P-38, at maximum cruising speed, was jumped by the Fw 190 and the Spitfire from about 1,500 ft above. The evasive action taken by the P-38 was to go into a shallow turning dive and gain speed. This appeared to be very effective against the Fw 190 because, although it had an initial advantage by diving 1,500 ft it was thought that a very long distance would be required to close to firing range as the P-38 gained speed very quickly, and when it was pulling up out of the dive it was found impossible for the Fw 190 to follow. The Spitfire IX was able to follow the P-38 in its pullout and turned inside it.

Performance:

Fw 190 *v* P-38. The two aircraft were compared for speed and all-round manoeuvrability at heights up to 23,000 ft. The Fw 190 was superior in speed at all heights up to 22,000 ft, where the two aircraft were approximately the same. The difference in speed decreased as the P-38F gained altitude until at 23,000 ft it was slightly faster. The difference in speeds were: at 2,000 ft, Fw 190 15 mph faster; at 8,000 ft, Fw 190 15 mph faster; at 15,000 ft, Fw 190 5 to 8 mph faster; at 23,000 ft, P-38F 6 to 8 mph faster than the Fw 190.

Climb:

The climb of the P-38 was not as good as that of the Fw 190 up to about 15,000 ft. Above this height the climb of the P-38 improved rapidly until at 20,000 ft it became superior. The best climbing speed of the P-38 was about 20 mph less than that of the Fw 190 but the angle was approximately the same. The initial rate of climb of the Fw 190 either from level flight or a dive was superior to that of the P-38 at all heights below 20,000 ft, and above this height, the climb of the P-38 became increasingly better.

Dive:

Comparative dives between the two aircraft proved the Fw 190 to be the better, particularly in the initial stages. During prolonged dives the P-38, on occasion, was catching up slightly, but during actual combat it was unlikely that the P-38 would have time to catch up before having to break off the attack.

Manoeuvrability:

The manoeuvrability of the Fw 190 was superior to that of the P-38, particularly in the rolling plane. Although at high speed the Fw 190 was superior in turning circles, it could be out-turned if the P-38 reduced its speed to about 140 mph, at which speed it could make a very tight turn which the Fw 190 could not follow. The acceleration of the two aircraft was compared and the Fw 190 was found to be better in all respects. When the Fw 190 'bounced' the P-38 and was seen when over 1,000 yards away, the pilot's best manoeuvre was to go into a diving turn and if it was found that the Fw 190 was catching up, to pull into a spiral climb, flying at the lowest possible speed. Although time did not permit trials to be made with the Fw 190 being 'bounced' by the P-38, it was thought the latter would stand a reasonable chance of shooting down the Fw 190 provided it had a slight height advantage and the element of surprise. If the pilot of the Fw 190 saw the P-38 when it was just out of range, a quick turn in one direction followed by a diving turn in the opposite direction would give the P-38 a most difficult target, and as acceleration and speed of the Fw 190 in a dive built up rapidly, it was likely to be able to dive away out of range.

Focke-Wulf Fw 190A-5/U8 PM679

Comparative trials flown at the AFDU, RAF Wittering, in 1943 against a Mustang III.

Maximum speed:

The Fw 190 was nearly 50 mph slower at most heights, and 70 mph slower above 28,000 ft.

Climb:

There appeared to be little to choose in the maximum rate of climb, but the Mustang was considerably faster at all heights in a zoom climb.

Dive:

The Mustang could always out-dive the Fw 190.

Turning circle:

Again, there was not much to choose but the Mustang was slightly better. When evading an enemy aircraft with a steep turn, a pilot could always out-turn the attacking aircraft initially because of the difference in speeds. It was therefore still a worthwhile manoeuvre when the Mustang was attacked.

Rate of roll:

Not even a Mustang approached the Fw 190.

Conclusions:

In the attack, a high speed had to be maintained or regained in order to regain the height initiative. The Fw 190 could not evade by diving alone. In defence a steep turn followed by a full throttle dive would increase the range before regaining height and course. Dog-fighting was not altogether recommended. No attempt was to be made to climb away without at least 250 mph showing initially.

Combat performance of the Mustang equipped with long-range tanks.
Speed:

There was a serious loss of speed of 40 to 50 mph at all engine settings and heights, but the Mustang was still faster than the Fw 190 above 25,000 ft.
Climb:

The Mustang was outclimbed by the Fw 190 and the rate of climb was greatly reduced. The Mustang was still good in a zoom climb, but was still outstripped when followed all the way by the Fw 190.
Dive:

So long as the tanks were fairly full, the Mustang still beat the Fw 190 in a power dive.
Turning circle:

The tanks did not make quite so much difference as one might have expected. The Mustang could at least turn as tightly as the Fw 190 without stalling out.
Rate of roll:

General handling and rate of roll was very little affected.
Conclusions:

The performance of the Mustang was greatly reduced when carrying drop-tanks. It was still a good attacking aircraft, especially if it had the advantage of height over the Fw 190.

Junkers Ju 88R-1 PJ876

Comparative trials were flown at the RAE Farnborough and RAF Hartford Bridge in 1943 to evaluate the FuG 202 Lichtenstein BC radar, and included mock combat against a Halifax of the Bomber Development Unit. As a night fighter it was noted, by Sq Ldr Hartley; 'At the heights tested, between 11,000 and 14,000 ft, this particular aircraft is less efficient than the Beaufighter VI with Mk.IV AI radar, although it is more pleasant to handle and may prove to be faster. The majority of its defects, *ie* cramped layout, lack of a broad windscreen and poor visibility, are traceable to its dive-bomber origin. The absence of a large flat windscreen makes itself felt when flying at night. The pilot always has the impression of peering out between prison bars, and his vision through any one panel is limited. The excellent handling qualities of this aircraft are to a considerable extent offset in night combat by the poor visibility from the pilot's seat. Provided the target can be viewed through either the left or right front panel, it is easily seen, but it is very much harder to see through the curved panels below these. When following a violently manoeuvring bomber the pilot is forced to place his head in unnatural and uncomfortable positions in an attempt to keep the bomber silhouette in the most favourable panel. The left hand front panel is the most satisfactory, but it is small, and is partially obstructed by the sight. Failure to keep the silhouette in this panel results in temporary loss of the visual target while it passes behind a "prison bar", and often in permanent loss if the range is long. The limitations of vision and the positioning of the sight close to one of the "prison bars" will make deflection shooting, particularly in right hand turns, even harder than is usual at night'. The Lichtenstein BC radar was found to be roughly comparable with the British AI Mk.IV, though the more cumbersome aerial system used with the German set produced a narrower beam, which made it easier to follow small movements by the target. Other RAF pilots who flew this aircraft were impressed by the quality of the gyro compass and artificial horizon.

Heinkel He 111H-1 AW177

Handling tests at the RAE in 1941, at 21,000 lb all-up weight: The take-off was quite straightforward with no tendency to swing and the initial and final climb were what could be expected from an aircraft of this size and power. The best approach speed was about 95 mph, there being an impression of sinking at 88 mph and of diving at 105 mph, flaps and undercarriage down. Stalling speed was 96 mph flaps up and 83 mph flaps down. Landing was simple and straightforward, even an indifferent landing seemed good as the aircraft was difficult to bounce and there was no tendency to swing during the ground run, which was rather long. Although the view from the cockpit was excellent taxi-ing was difficult, the toe brakes being awkward to operate and heavy pressure was needed to get the desired braking effect. The aircraft could be trimmed to fly straight and level on one engine with feet and hands off. The controls were reasonably well harmonized at cruising speed, becoming rather heavy in the dive, but showing no abnormalities.

Junkers Ju 88A-5 EE205

Handling tests at the RAE in 1941: The aircraft had to be taxied straight just before opening the throttles in order to lock the tailwheel in the correct fore and aft position, and provided the throttles were opened slowly and evenly the tendency to swing was not very marked. Above 50 mph the rudder became very effective, although the aircraft did not readily fly itself off, the control column having to be pulled back firmly to unstick. Take-off run was rather long, but speed built up rapidly once off the ground giving full control in a short space of time, the undercarriage retracting in 12 seconds. Maximum speed was about 290 mph without external bomb load and 270 mph with, top speeds being obtained at 15,000 ft. Service ceiling at 28,000 lb all-up weight was 24,000 ft. On the approach the undercarriage had to be lowered at 2,000 ft, a certain amount of engine normally being used. If the engines were throttled right back the best approach speed was 115 mph, at 105 mph there was a sensation of sinking and at 125 mph one of diving. Stalling speed was 93 mph with flaps down and 116 mph with flaps up, although on lowering the flaps control in general felt more sloppy but was quite adequate on the glide. The Ju 88 was not easy to land, it was difficult to get the tail fully down and the brakes had to be used with caution, while there was a tendency to swing after touch-down which had to be immediately corrected. The aircraft handled well while taxi-ing, the brakes being particularly effective. The Ju 88 was obviously an extremely useful aircraft with good performance and load carrying qualities combined with excellent manoeuvrability for its size at high speeds; however it was not an easy aircraft to operate mainly owing to its high loading. Inexperienced pilots in particular had to take some time to get used to the approach and landing, especially with one engine inoperative. Its reputation as a somewhat tricky aircraft may be clearly discerned from the following quotation taken from the official D(Luft) T Handbook: 'Because of its special purposes as bomber and dive-bomber the type Ju 88 had to follow constructional principles which show several changes from what was normal hitherto. If the pilot bears this carefully in mind the 88 presents no special difficulty, on the contrary the pilot, after gaining experience, feels very comfortable even under difficult conditions and is enthusiastic about the fighting power of his aircraft'.

Messerschmitt Bf 110C-5 AX772

Handling tests at the RAE in the summer of 1941: The take-off run was rather long and rudder had to be used coarsely to prevent swing in the early stages. Optimum flap setting at the weight tested, 13,000 lb, was 20 deg and at this setting little effort was required to unstick, whereas with flaps up considerable forward force was needed to get the tail up. The initial climb was excellent and control adequate during the climb. Top speed was 340 mph at 22,000 ft, rate of climb being 2,200 ft a minute at 5,000 ft and 1,500 ft a minute at 20,000 ft, while service ceiling was 33,000 ft. The best approach speed, flaps and undercarriage down, was about 95 mph, but on lowering the flaps there was a very large change of attitude. At the beginning of the flap movement the nose came up and a large forward stick force was needed to counteract this, towards the end of the flap movement the nose sank requiring a slight pull to maintain the speed, the eventual change of trim being small. The flaps took 7 seconds to come fully down at 110 mph. The longitudinal stability on the glide was exceptionally good and pilots considered this an excellent feature, since once the aeroplane was trimmed there was little need to watch the ASI closely. View during the approach was excellent and the landing itself very straightforward and easy, with no tendency for a wing to drop, and heavy braking could be used during the ground run without fear of lifting the tail. Ground handling qualities were very satisfactory, the aircraft being easily controlled by use of the engines or brakes, which were operated by toe pedals, and there was excellent view while taxi-ing. The consensus of opinion was that the Bf 110 was a very pleasant aircraft for normal flying, but that its handling qualities as a military aircraft left much to be desired, mainly due to its lack of manoeuvrability at medium and high airspeeds. Its wing loading of 33 lb/sq ft, allowing a level turning circle of 1,000 ft, gave it an advantage in a slow-speed circling dog-fight against a more heavily loaded twin but against single-engined fighters, of about 25 lb/sq ft wing loading, it had neither advantage of turning circle at low airspeeds nor of manoeuvrability at high airspeeds.

Pilots' Log Book Extracts

Flight Lieutenant D. G. M. Gough, No. 1426 (EAC) Flight

DATE	AIRCRAFT	REMARKS
3 Nov 1941	He 111H-1 AW177	Experience flight on type
2 Jan 1942	Bf 109E-3 AE479	Experience flight on type
9 Jan 1942	Ju 88 A-5 HM509	Experience flight on type
11 Feb 1942	Ju 88A-5 HM509	From Duxford to Leconheath for demonstration
17 Feb 1942	He 111H-1 AW177	Coltishall and Bircham Newton, with 10 passengers!
24 March 1942	Bf 109E-3 DG200	A & E test
1 April 1942	Bf 110C-5 AX772	Duxford to North Luffenham
25 April 1942	He 111H-1 AW177	Air test
8 May 1942	Ju 88A-5 HM509	Air test
1 June 1942	Bf 109E-3 DG200	Air test
19 June 1942	Bf 110C-5 AX772	Air test
19 June 1942	Bf 109E-3 DG200	Duxford to Stradishall
28 June 1942	He111H-1 AW177	Demonstration at Duxford with Wing Cmdr B. E. 'Paddy' Finucane plus 13 other passengers
30 June 1942	Bf 109E-3 DG200	To Detling for demonstration
6 Aug 1942	Ju 88A-5 HM509	To A & AEE, Boscombe Down
12 Aug 1942	He 111H-1 AW177	Handling trials
17 Oct 1942	Ju 88A-5 EE205	Demonstration flight
27 Oct 1942	Ju 88A-5 EE205	From Exeter to the RAE
3 Nov 1942	Ju 88A-5 EE205	Dive bombing tests for RN Film Unit
8 Nov 1942	Ju 88A-5 EE205	Affiliation exercises with No. 502 Squadron, St Eval
8 Nov 1942	Ju 88A-5 EE205	Air test, tail locking u/s
24 Nov 1942	Ju 88A-5 EE205	Affiliation exercises with No. 235 Squadron, Chivenor
26 Jan 1943	Bf 110C-5 AX772	A & E test
20 Feb 1943	Ju 88A-5 HM509	A & E test
26 June 1943	Ju 88A-5 HM509	Affiliation exercises with a Lancaster
3 July 1943	Ju 88A-5 HM509	Affiliation with Wellington
17 Aug 1943	He 111H-1 AW177	Instructional film for Army Film Unit
1 Oct 1943	Fw 190A-4 PN999	Handling trials
4 Oct 1943	He 111H-1 AW177	BBC sound recording engineers on board

9 Oct 1943	Fw 190A-4 PN999	Local test flying
10 Nov 1943	Bf 109F-4/B NN644	To Grafton Underwood and Polebrook
3 Jan 1944	Bf 109F-4/B NN644	Photographic and demonstration session, Collyweston
29 Feb 1944	Bf 109G-2/Trop RN228	Comparative trials with Corsair
1 March 1944	Bf 109G-2/Trop RN228	Comparative trials with Seafire
23 March 1944	Fw 190A-4 PN999	Comparative trials with Spitfire
7 April 1944	Bf 109G-2/Trop RN228	Flight to Andrews Field but force-landed at Rivenhall
23 April 1944	Bf 109G-6/Trop VX101	To Wattisham and Boxted
9 May 1944	Ju 88A-5 HM509	Collyweston to Thorney Island
19 May 1944	Fw 190A-4/U8 PE882	Demonstration flight from Thorney Island, landed Ford
14 June 1944	Ju 88R-1 PJ876	Thorney Island to Holmsley South
15 June 1944	Fw 190A-4 PN999	From Holmsley South to Collyweston
25–27 July 1944	Ju 88R-1 PJ876	Bombing and photographic sessions for Realist Film Co film *Tinker Tailor*
11 Aug 1944	Bf 109G-2/Trop RN228	Little Snoring to Massingham
5 Sept 1944	Ju 88R-1 PJ876	A & E test
27 Oct 1944	Hs 129B-1 NF756	Experience flight on type
2 Nov 1944	Ju 88S-1 TS472	A & E test
9 Feb 1945	Bf 109G-14/U4 VD364	From Deurne to Hawkinge
24 Feb 1945	Ju 88A-5 EE205	Instructional flight
24 Feb 1945	Fw 190A-4 PN999	A & E test
24 March 1945	Bf 109G-14/U4 VD358	From Hawkinge to Tangmere
27 March 1945	Bf 109G-2/Trop RN228	From Collyweston to Tangmere
3 April 1945	Fw 190A-4 PN999	Air test
18 April 1945	Ju 88S-1 TS472	Collyweston to Tangmere
1 May 1945	Fw 190A-4 PN999	Tangmere to Old Sarum, demonstration and return
4 May 1945	Ju 88R-1 PJ876	Collyweston to Tangmere
29 May 1945	Fi 156	Local flying at Leck
31 May 1945	Si 204	Luttenholm–Schleswig–Leck
7 June 1945	Ju 88G-6 CB	Gilze-Rijen to Tangmere
12 June 1945	Ju 88G-6 Air Min 32	Air test
13 June 1945	Ju 88G-6 Air Min 31	Air test
14 June 1945	Ju 52/3m GD1	Schleswig to Eggebeck
14 June 1945	Ju 88G-6 Air Min 15	Eggebeck to Schleswig
16 June 1945	Ju 88G-6 Air Min 1	Air test
16 June 1945	Ju 88G-6 Air Min 16	Schleswig to Tangmere
22 June 1945	Bf 108 Air Min 76	Air test
12 July 1945	Fw 190A-4 PN999	Airframe test, tailplane change
27 Aug 1945	Fw 190A-4 PN999	Engine test, fractured oil line
25 Sept 1945	Ju 88G-6 Air Min 32	A & E test, then to West Raynham
11 Oct 1945	Ju 88G-1 TP190	Air test

Captain Eric Brown, CBE, DSC, AFC, RN, CO Aerodynamics Flight, Royal Aircraft Establishment, Farnborough

DATE	AIRCRAFT	REMARKS
25 Aug 1944	Bf 109G-6/U2 TP814	Air test
20 Sept 1944	He 177A-5/R6 TS439	Air test
2 June 1945	Ju 88G-7a VK888	Gormanstown, Eire, to the RAE
25 June 1945	Ar 234B-1 VK880	Karup (Grove) to the RAE, via Schleswig
18 July 1945	Ju 188 c/n 150245	—
26 July 1945	Ju 52/3m D-AGAC	RAE to No. 6 MU Brize Norton
28 July 1945	Fw 190F-8 Air Min 111	Air test
1 Aug 1945	DFS Meise LF-VO	Air test
14 Aug 1945	Bf 108 GJ-AU	RAE to No. 6 MU Brize Norton
17 Aug 1945	Ju 290A-7 c/n 0186	RAE to No. 6 MU Brize Norton
18 Aug 1945	Ta 152H-1 c/n 150168	Air test
19 Aug 1945	Si 204D c/n 221558	RAE to Thorney Island
21 Aug 1945	He 219A-2 c/n 290126	RAE to No. 6 MU Brize Norton
30 Aug 1945	Ju 88 c/n 622811	RAE to No. 6 MU Brize Norton
30 Aug 1945	Ju 88G-6 VL991	RAE, instrument flying
5 Sept 1945	Bf 110G-4/R3 c/n 730301	RAE to No. 6 MU Brize Norton
5 Sept 1945	Fw 190S-8 Air Min 29	RAE to No. 6 MU Brize Norton
6 Sept 1945	Me 262A c/n 500200	Manston to the RAE
7 Sept 1945	He 162A-2 Air Min 67	Air test
7 Sept 1945	Ar 234B-1 VH530	RAE to No. 6 MU Brize Norton
8 Sept 1945	Ju 188A-2 VN143	RAE to Gosport
7 Oct 1945	Ar 234B c/n 140356	Brussels (Melsbroek) to the RAE
17 Oct 1945	Ju 88G-1 TP190	From Tangmere to the RAE
18 Oct 1945	Do 217M-1 Air Min 107	Handling trials, RAE
18 Dec 1945	Ju 88 c/n 0660	RAE to Gosport
21 Dec 1945	Me 410A-1 c/n 10360	RAE to No. 6 MU Brize Norton
16 Jan 1946	Bü 181C-3 Air Min 122	—
18 Jan 1946	Fw 189A-3 Air Min 27	RAE to No. 6 MU Brize Norton
8 March 1946	Ju 352A-1 Air Min 8	—
18 April 1946	Fw 58 LO-WQ	—
28 May 1946	Fi 156C-1 VP546	RNAS Ford to HMS *Triumph*
29 May 1946	Fi 156C-1 VP546	HMS *Triumph* to the RAE
13 May 1947	Ho IV LA-AC	RAE
1 Sept 1947	DFS Kranich 2 VP591	—
18 Sept 1947	Zaunkönig D-YBAR	RAE, first flight in UK
30 Sept 1947	Me 163B-1a VF241	Test flight, Wisley
1 Nov 1947	Me 163B-1a VF241	Wisley to Wittering, towed by Spitfire LF.IX

Air Commodore A. H. Wheeler, CBE, MA, FRAeS, CO Experimental Flight, Royal Aircraft Establishment, Farnborough 1942–44

DATE	AIRCRAFT	REMARKS
25 April 1942	Ju 88A-5 EE205?	—
12 July 1942	Fw 190A-3 MP499	Caused a lot of anxiety to our fighter pilots, after capture and testing proved to have been nothing like as frightening as we thought it was. It took us a long time getting it flying because it was all electric and the electrics gave trouble. Also, one of the brakes wouldn't work until we found that the German mechanics had assembled it wrong—one worked and one didn't. The engine was appalling and always seemed as though it was just going to blow up, during the later stages of our tests it did!
12 Aug 1942	Bf 110C-5 AX772	—
12 Aug 1942	Bf 109E-3/B DG200	Had no hood on so it was difficult to assess its suitability as a fighter since without the hood it had a definite speed limitation and, in any case, the noise and disturbance in the cockpit was distracting.
21 May 1943	Fw 190A-4/U8 PE882	—
18 Aug 1949	Fi 156 VX154	In general all German aeroplanes seemed much heavier with an apparently higher wing loading than ours and they always gave the impression that if one allowed them to, they would come back on to the ground like a ton of bricks. This was even true of the Storch which was supposed to be a slow flying type but I always considered it dangerous, particularly at the slow end of the speed range and, in fact, it proved to be dangerous on a number of occasions.